Independent Technical Review and Analysis of Hydraulic Modeling and Hydrology Under Low-Flow Conditions of the Des Plaines River Near Riverside, Illinois

By Thomas M. Over, Timothy D. Straub, Jon E. Hortness, and Elizabeth A. Murphy

Open-File Report 2012–1143

U.S. Department of the Interior
U.S. Geological Survey

U.S. Department of the Interior
KEN SALAZAR, Secretary

U.S. Geological Survey
Marcia K. McNutt, Director

U.S. Geological Survey, Reston, Virginia: 2012

For more information on the USGS—the Federal source for science about the Earth, its natural and living resources, natural hazards, and the environment, visit http://www.usgs.gov or call 1–888–ASK–USGS.

For an overview of USGS information products, including maps, imagery, and publications, visit http://www.usgs.gov/pubprod

To order this and other USGS information products, visit http://store.usgs.gov

Suggested citation:
Over, T.M., Straub, T.D., Hortness, J.E., and Murphy, E.A., 2012, Independent technical review and analysis of hydraulic modeling and hydrology under low-flow conditions of the Des Plaines River near Riverside, Illinois: U.S. Geological Survey Open-File Report 2012–1143, 73 p.

Contents

Conversion Factors and Abbreviations

Inch/Pound to SI

Multiply	By	To obtain
Length		
foot (ft)	0.3048	meter (m)
mile (mi)	1.609	kilometer (km)
Area		
square mile (mi²)	259.0	hectare (ha)
square mile (mi²)	2.590	square kilometer (km²)
Flow rate		
cubic foot per second (ft³/s or cfs)	0.02832	cubic meter per second (m³/s)

Vertical coordinate information is referenced to the North American Vertical Datum of 1988 (NAVD 88).

Abbreviations

+/−	Plus or minus
%	Percent
7Q10	7-day annual minimum discharge with 10-year return period
Addison.Ck	Addison Creek at Bellwood, Illinois
Ck	Creek
CY	Calendar year
DPR	Des Plaines River
DPR.abvSalt.DAadj	Des Plaines River above Salt Creek with adjustment of discharge for ungaged drainage area
DPR.abvSalt.noDAadj	Des Plaines River above Salt Creek without adjustment of discharge for ungaged drainage area
DPR.abvSalt.MWRDdiv.DAadj	Des Plaines River above Salt Creek with Salt Creek diversion computed with MWRD rating and with adjustment of Salt Creek discharge for ungaged drainage area
DPR.abvSalt.MWRDdiv.noDAadj	Des Plaines River above Salt Creek with Salt Creek diversion computed with MWRD rating and without adjustment of Salt Creek discharge for ungaged drainage area
DPR.DesPlaines	Des Plaines River near Des Plaines, Illinois
GPS	Global positioning system
HEC-RAS	Hydrologic Engineering Center-River Analysis System

IDNR	Illinois Department of Natural Resources
ISWS	Illinois State Water Survey
MWRD	Metropolitan Water Reclamation District of Greater Chicago
N/A	Not available
OLS	Ordinary least squares
OWR	Office of Water Resources
Q7	7-day annual minimum discharge
SaltCk.at.div.DAadj	Salt Creek at diversion with adjustment of discharge for ungaged drainage area
SaltCk.at.div.noDAadj	Salt Creek at diversion without adjustment of discharge for ungaged drainage area
SaltCk.MWRDdiv.DAadj	Salt Creek diversion computed with MWRD rating with adjustment of discharge of Salt Creek at diversion for ungaged drainage area
SaltCk.MWRDdiv.noDAadj	Salt Creek diversion computed with MWRD rating without adjustment of discharge of Salt Creek at diversion for ungaged drainage area
SaltCk.WSprings	Salt Creek at Western Springs, Illinois.
USACE	U.S. Army Corps of Engineers
WWTP	Wastewater Treatment Plant
WY	Water year

Independent Technical Review and Analysis of Hydraulic Modeling and Hydrology Under Low-Flow Conditions of the Des Plaines River Near Riverside, Illinois

By Thomas M. Over, Timothy D. Straub, Jon E. Hortness, and Elizabeth A. Murphy

Introduction

The U.S. Geological Survey (USGS) has operated a streamgage and published daily flows for the Des Plaines River at Riverside since Oct. 1, 1943. A HEC-RAS model has been developed to estimate the effect of the removal of Hofmann Dam near the gage on low-flow elevations in the reach approximately 3 miles upstream from the dam. The Village of Riverside, the Illinois Department of Natural Resources-Office of Water Resources (IDNR-OWR), and the U. S. Army Corps of Engineers-Chicago District (USACE-Chicago) are interested in verifying the performance of the HEC-RAS model for specific low-flow conditions, and obtaining an estimate of selected daily flow quantiles and other low-flow statistics for a selected period of record that best represents current hydrologic conditions. Because the USGS publishes streamflow records for the Des Plaines River system and provides unbiased analyses of flows and stream hydraulic characteristics, the USGS served as an Independent Technical Reviewer (ITR) for this study.

≥USGS

science for a changing world

Independent Technical Review and Analysis of Hydraulic Modeling and Hydrology Under Low-Flow Conditions of the Des Plaines River Near Riverside, Illinois

U.S. Department of the Interior
U.S. Geological Survey

Background

- Hofmann Dam
  - Low-head dam on the Des Plaines River in Riverside
  - Constructed by the State of Illinois in 1950
  - The U. S. Army Corps of Engineers – Chicago District (USACE) has developed plans to remove the dam.

- HEC-RAS model
  - Developed by the U. S. Army Corps of Engineers – Chicago District
  - Model the effects of the removal of Hofmann Dam
  - Study area is Hofmann Dam to 26th Street (approximately 3 mi)

≥USGS

What is the USGS?

- **U.S. Geological Survey**
  - Department of Interior
  - Nation's largest earth science agency
  - No regulatory responsibility

- **Created by Congress in 1879**

- **Mission**
  - Provide the Nation with reliable, <u>impartial</u> information about the Earth
  - Data collection and interpretive projects

USGS

Streamflow Data within Area of Detailed Study

- ## USGS streamflow-gaging station 05532500 on Des Plaines River
  - Downstream of Hofmann Dam (Millbridge Road)
  - Continuous streamflow data since 1943

USGS

Components of the Technical Review/Analysis Under Low-Flow Conditions

- Field data collection

- Hydraulic model verification (using field data collected)

- Hydrology review/analysis

- Hydraulic model results (using flows determined in hydrologic analysis)

USGS

Study Area Map

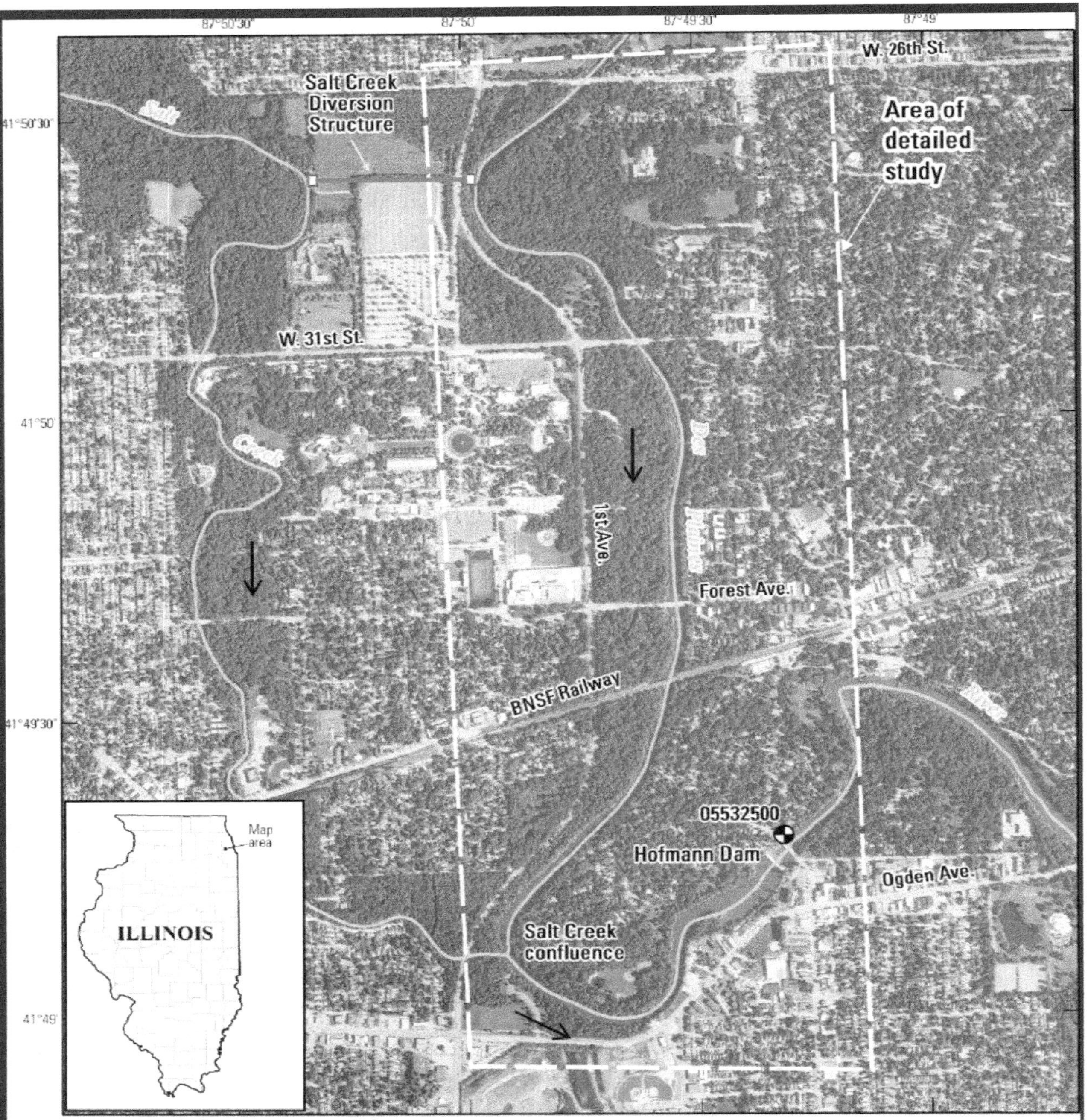

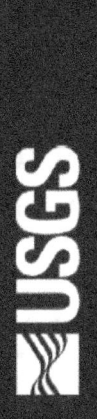

87°50'30"
87°50'
87°49'30"
87°49'
41°50'30"
41°50'
41°49'30"
41°49'
W. 26th St.
Salt Creek Diversion Structure
Area of detailed study
Salt
W. 31st St.
Creek
Des
Plaines
1st Ave.
Forest Ave.
BNSF Railway
River
05532500
Hofmann Dam
Ogden Ave.
Salt Creek confluence
Map area
ILLINOIS

Base imagery from USDA Farm Services Agency 2011 NAIP
Natural Color Imagery for Illinois acquired between August 2, 2011
and September 15, 2011. Accessed in June 2012 at:
http://gis.apfo.usda.gov/ArcGIS/services/NAIP/

0 0.5 MILE
0 0.5 KILOMETER

EXPLANATION

USGS streamflow-gaging station and number

Direction of flow

USGS

Field Data Collection
Under Low-Flow Conditions

- Flow measurements

- Water-surface elevations

- Manning's Roughness observations

Flow Measurements
(May 17, 2012)

- Measurement accuracy is +/-5%
- Measurement locations chosen to identify changes in flows
- Value at USGS streamflow-gaging station 05532500 is average of two measurements (made at beginning and end of data collection)

≊USGS

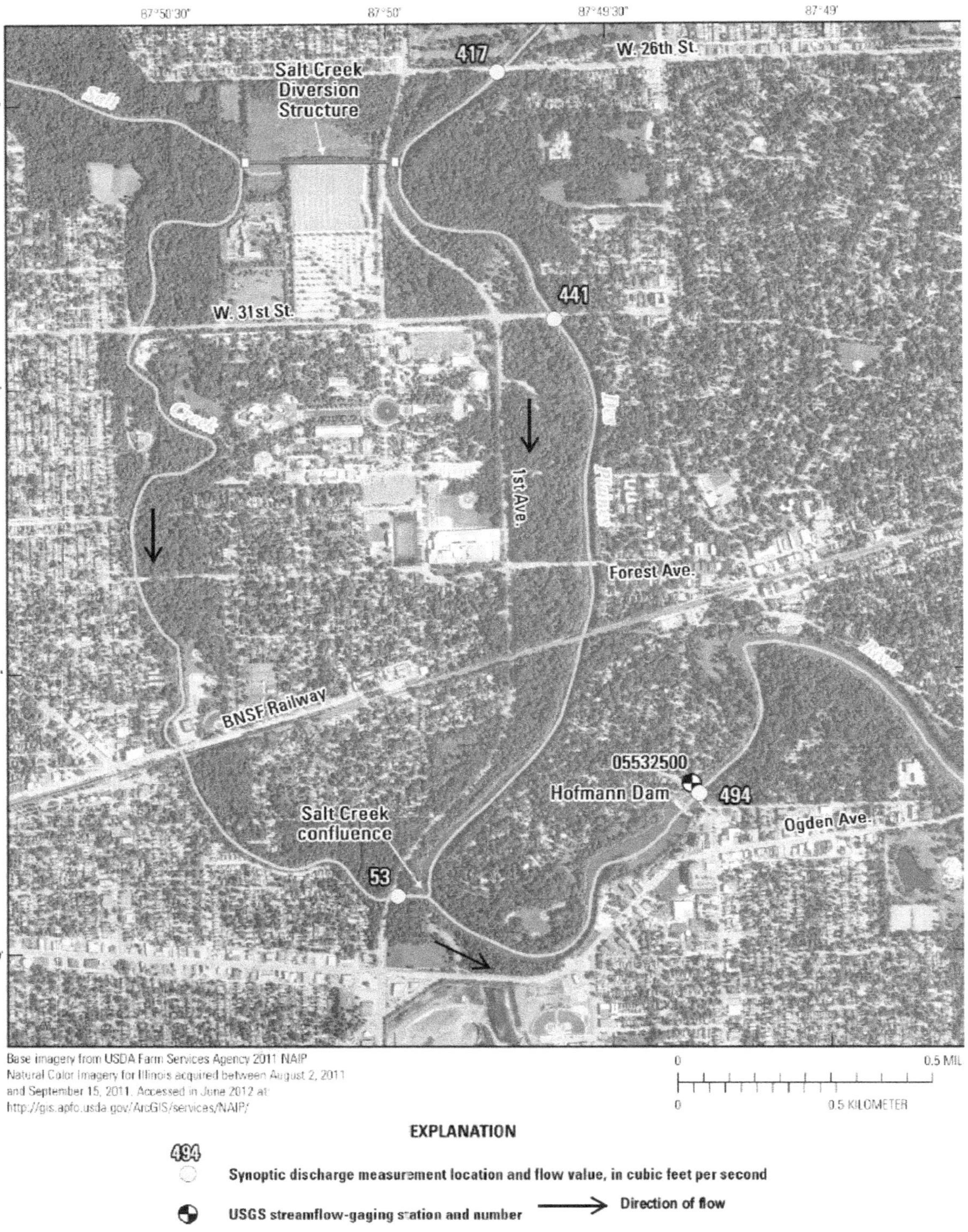

W. 26th St.

W. 31st St.

1st Ave.

Forest Ave.

Salt Creek
Diversion
Structure

BNSF Railway

Salt Creek
confluence

Hofmann Dam

Ogden Ave.

Des Plaines

417

441

494

53

05532500

Base imagery from USDA Farm Services Agency 2011 NAIP
Natural Color Imagery for Illinois acquired between August 2, 2011
and September 15, 2011. Accessed in June 2012 at
http://gis.apfo.usda.gov/ArcGIS/services/NAIP/

0   0.5 MILE
0   0.5 KILOMETER

EXPLANATION

494 (○) Synoptic discharge measurement location and flow value, in cubic feet per second

→ Direction of flow

◉ USGS streamflow-gaging station and number

Salt Creek Diversion Structure

- Constructed in 1960
  - Inlet modified in 1967
- Main purpose: flood protection along Lower Salt Creek
- Flow in the diversion is controlled by the water level of Salt Creek

Flow from diversion structure into Des Plaines River 05/17/2012 12:51

Flow from Salt Creek into diversion structure

Water-Surface Elevations (May 17, 2012)

- **GPS accuracy +/– 0.07 ft**

- **Small errors possible due to difficulties holding equipment at water surface**

- **Computed drop in water surface between 26th Street and Hofmann Dam was 0.92 ft**

≈USGS

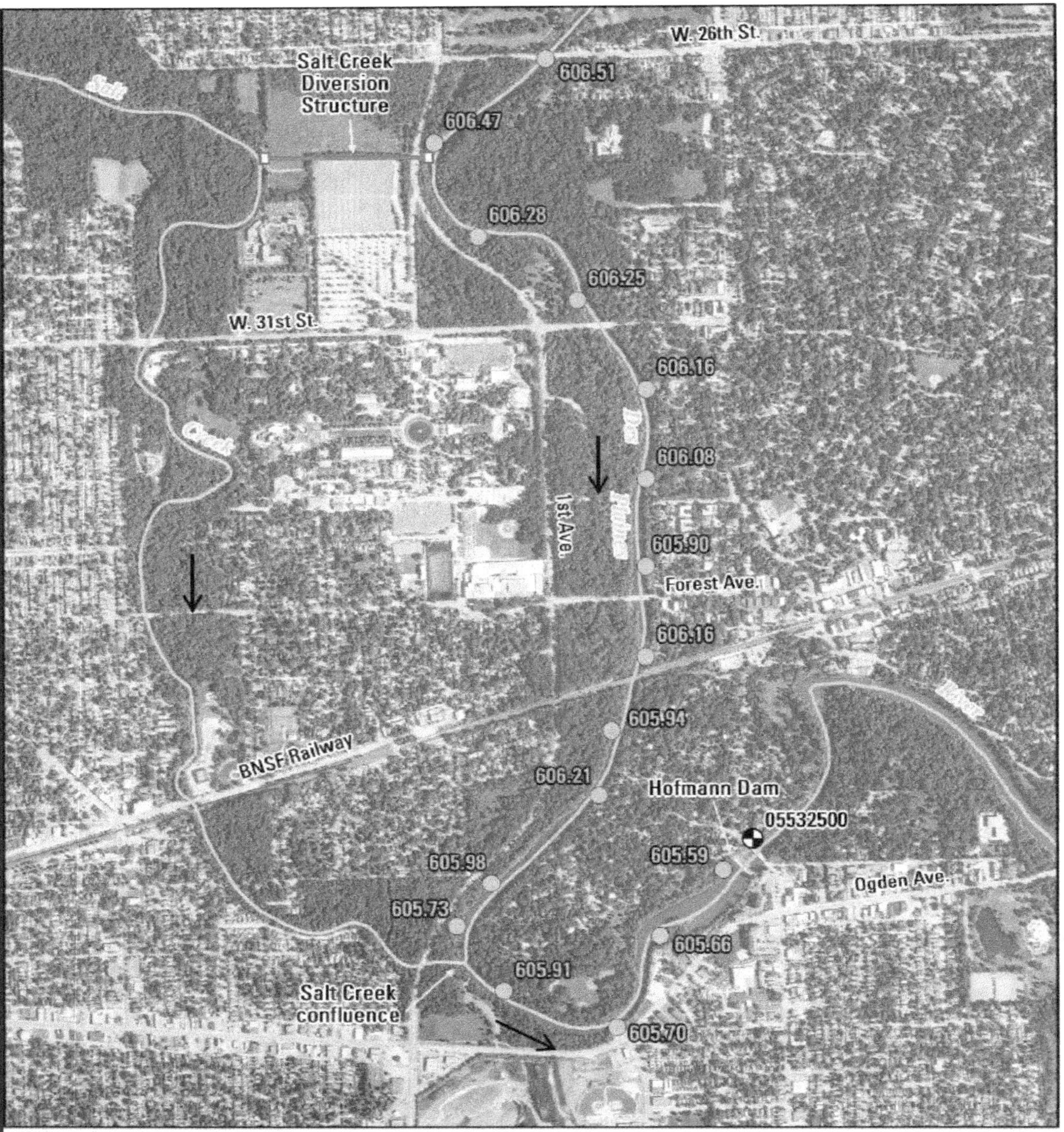

Base imagery from USDA Farm Services Agency 2011 NAIP
Natural Color Imagery for Illinois acquired between August 2, 2011
and September 15, 2011. Accessed in June 2012 at:
http://gis.apfo.usda.gov/ArcGIS/services/NAIP/

W. 26th St.

W. 31st St.

Salt Creek Diversion Structure

606.51
606.47
606.28
606.25
606.16
606.08
605.90
Forest Ave.
606.16
605.94
1st Ave.
Des Plaines
606.21
605.98
605.73
605.91
BNSF Railway
Hofmann Dam
05532500
605.59
605.66
Ogden Ave.
605.70
Salt Creek confluence

EXPLANATION

605.59 Synoptic water-surface sampling location elevation, in feet above NAVD88

⬤ USGS streamflow-gaging station and number

→ Direction of flow

0   0.5 MILE
0   0.5 KILOMETER

Manning's Roughness (n-value)

- A measure of flow resistance based on several factors including: channel material, channel shape, vegetation, etc.

- Used in hydraulic models to represent the resistance to flow in the channel

- Typical values in natural channels range from 0.025 to 0.070 (Chow, 1959)

USGS

Manning's Roughness: General Observations

- Bed material seems to be mainly fine-grained sands, silts, and clays.

- Most river banks are made up of silts and clays with minimal vegetation up to the floodplain.

  - Woody debris is common along many of the banks.

Manning's Roughness: Summary

- Manning's roughness in the study reach should likely range from approximately 0.035 to 0.045.

- These values are relevant for flows within the main channel; values during flood conditions would be substantially different.

USGS

Hydraulic Model Verification

- Comparison of modeled and observed water-surface elevations

- Manning's roughness sensitivity analysis

Observed Water Surface Locations and Corresponding Selected Model Cross Sections

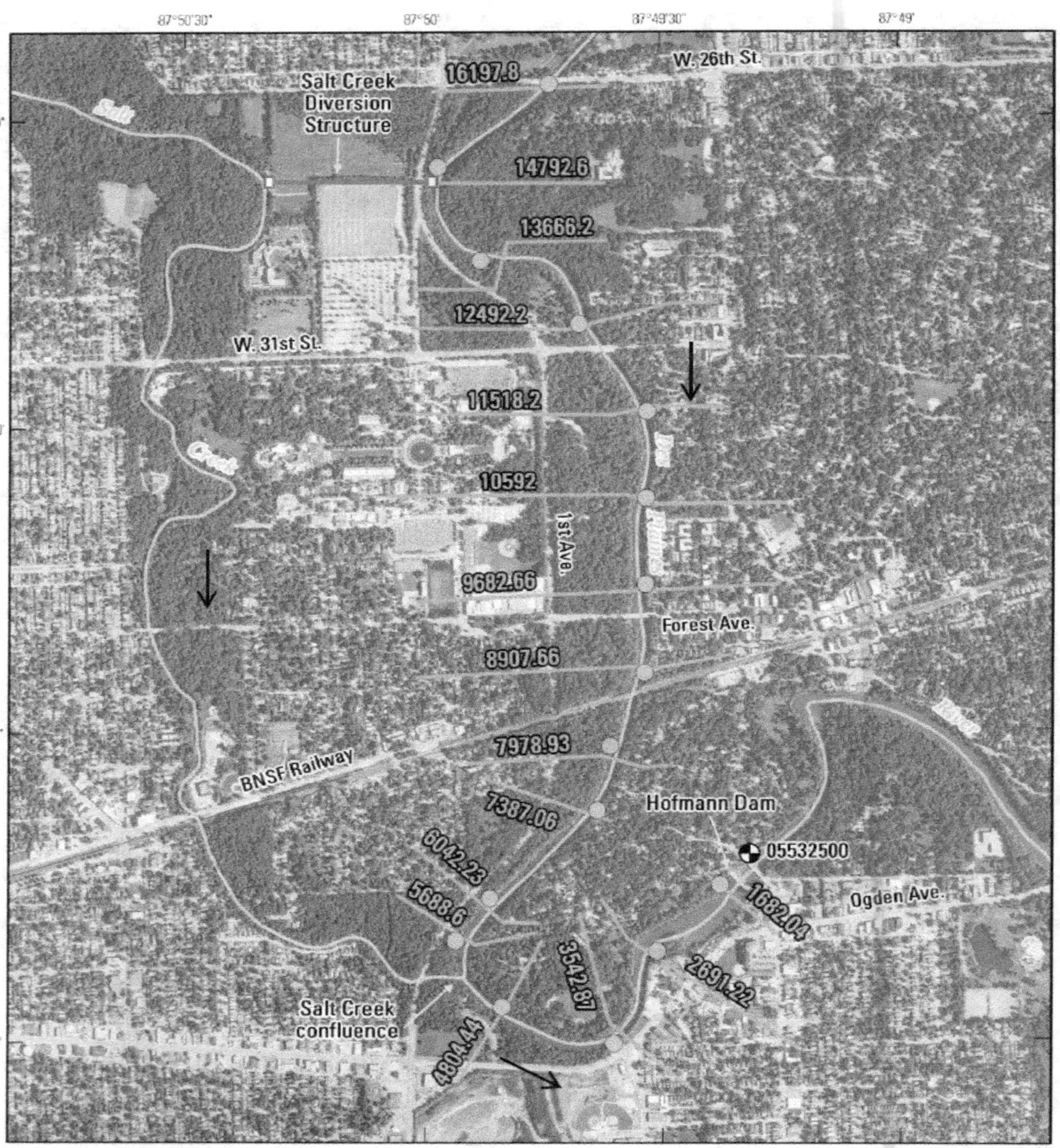

Base imagery from USDA Farm Services Agency 2011 NAIP
Natural Color Imagery for Illinois acquired between August 2, 2011
and September 15, 2011. Accessed in June 2012 at
http://gis.apfo.usda.gov/ArcGIS/services/NAIP/

EXPLANATION

○ Synoptic water-surface elevation location

◉ USGS streamflow-gaging station and number

— Synoptic cross section with river station label

→ Direction of flow

1682.04

W. 26th St.

W. 31st St.

1st Ave.

Forest Ave.

Des Plaines

Dam

Salt Creek
Diversion
Structure

Salt Creek
confluence

BNSF Railway

Hofmann Dam

Ogden Ave.

05532500

16197.8

14792.6

13666.2

12492.2

11511.82

10592

9662.66

8907.66

7978.93

7387.06

6042.23

5688.6

3542.87

2691.22

1682.04

4804.64

River

Creek

Salt

Creek

87°49'

87°49'30"

87°50'

87°50'30"

41°50'30"

41°50'

41°49'30"

41°49'

0   0.5 MILE

0   0.5 KILOMETER

Water Surface Elevations Modeled With Flows Measured on May 17, 2012

Manning's roughness = 0.035

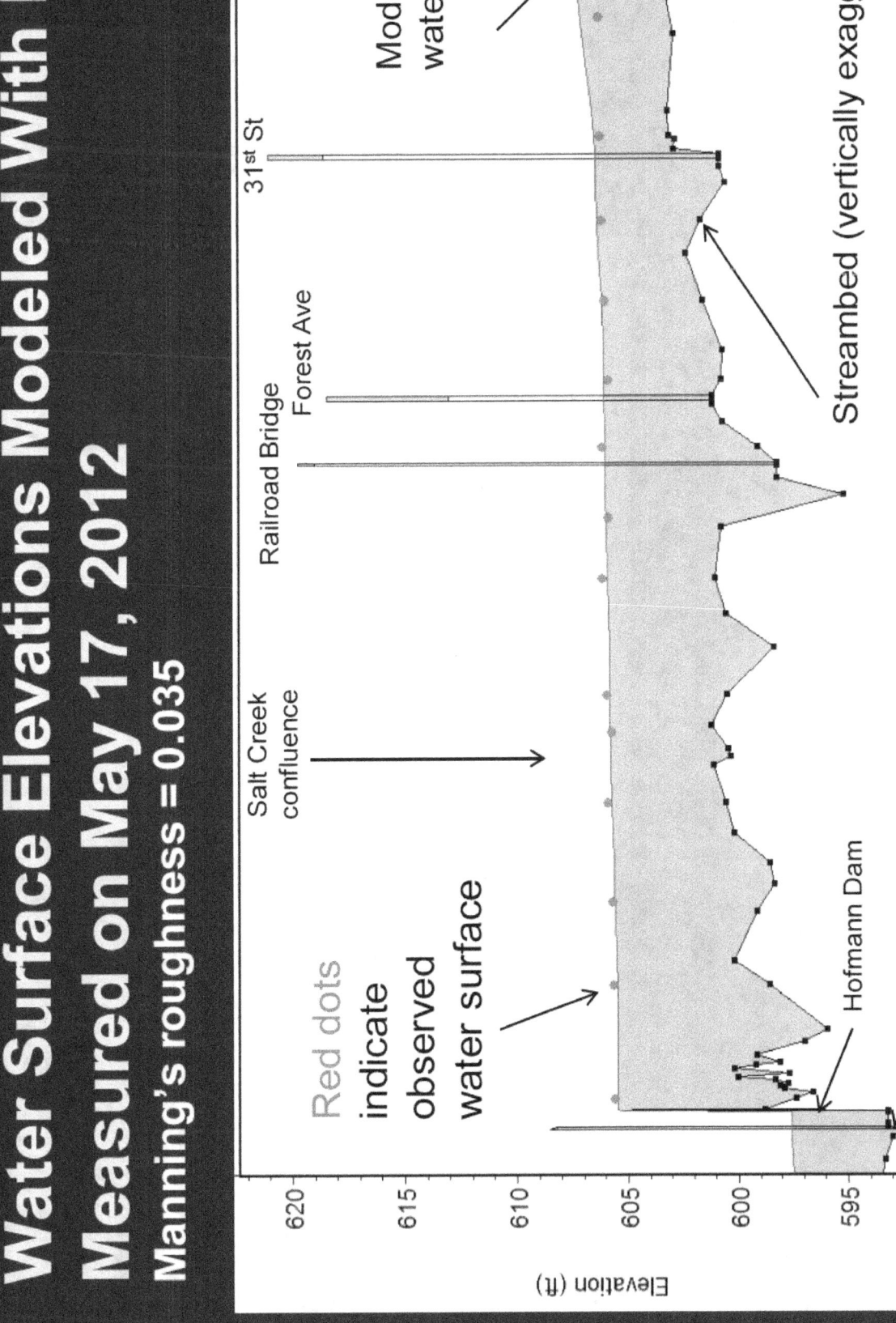

Comparison Among Manning's Roughness Coefficients

Main-channel Manning's roughness of 0.035 selected based on comparison of errors

Dam to 31st Street	
Manning's Roughness Coefficient	Error[1] (ft)
0.035	+/- 0.16
0.040	+/- 0.21
0.045	+/- 0.30

[1]Root mean square error

Observed Flows Modeled

Modeled with flows measured on May 17, 2012
Manning's roughness = 0.035

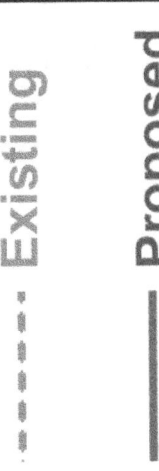

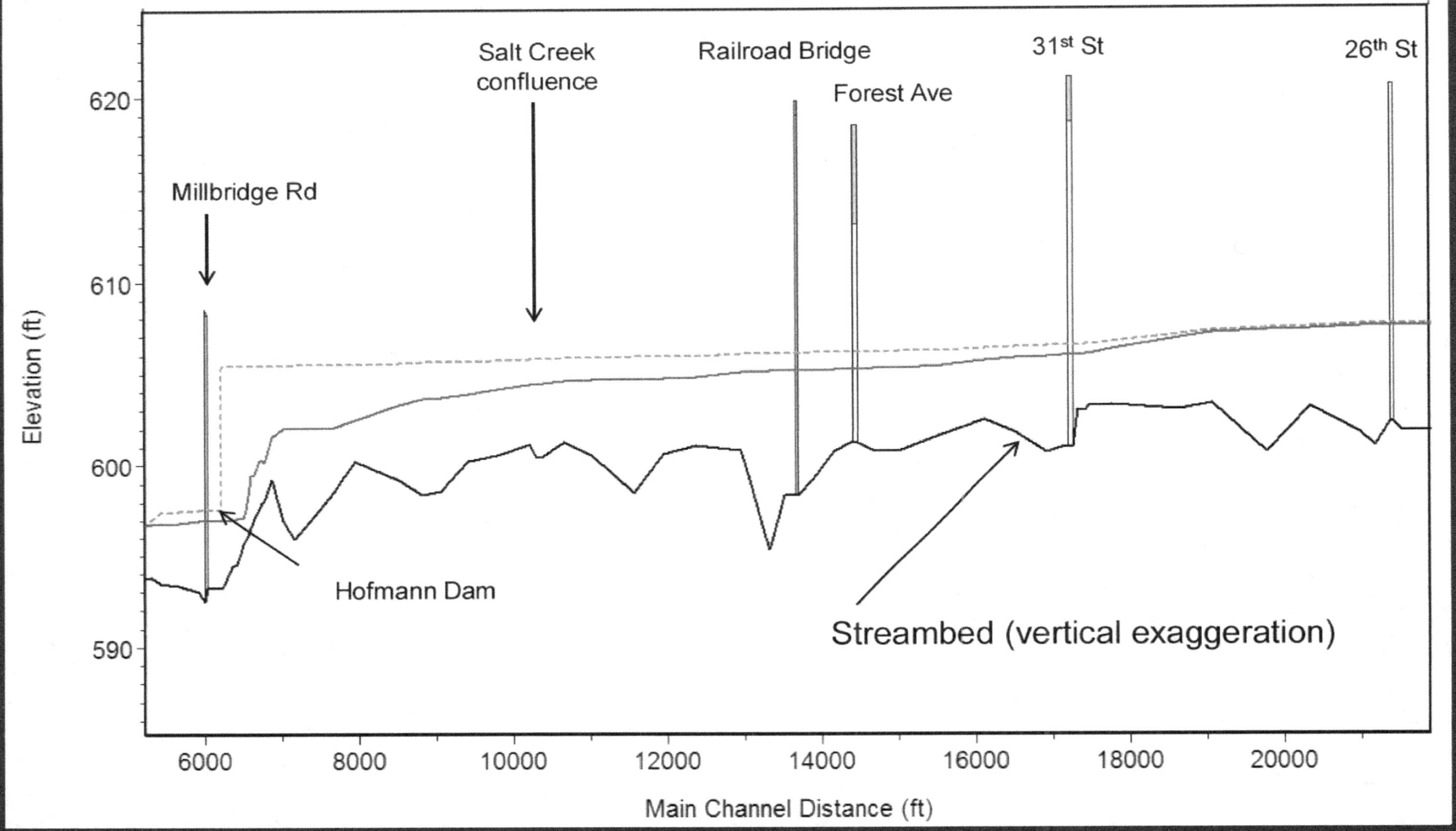

- - - - - Existing
———— Proposed

26th St

31st St

Railroad Bridge

Forest Ave

Salt Creek confluence

Millbridge Rd

Hofmann Dam

Streambed (vertical exaggeration)

Elevation (ft)

620
610
600
590

Main Channel Distance (ft)

6000   8000   10000   12000   14000   16000   18000   20000

Hydrology Review/Analysis

- **Purpose: Compute flow statistics for use in hydraulic modeling**

- **Overview of tasks**
  - Computation of daily flows
  - Trend analyses of flow statistics to determine appropriate period of record
  - Computation of flow statistics

Flow Statistics Computed

- Daily flows with 80% (low), 50%, and 20% exceedance probabilities

  - 7Q10: annual 7-day minimum flow (Q7) with 10-year return period

➢ Only low flows results will be presented: 80% exceedance daily flow and 7Q10

Streamflow-gaging Stations and Des Plaines River Study Reaches

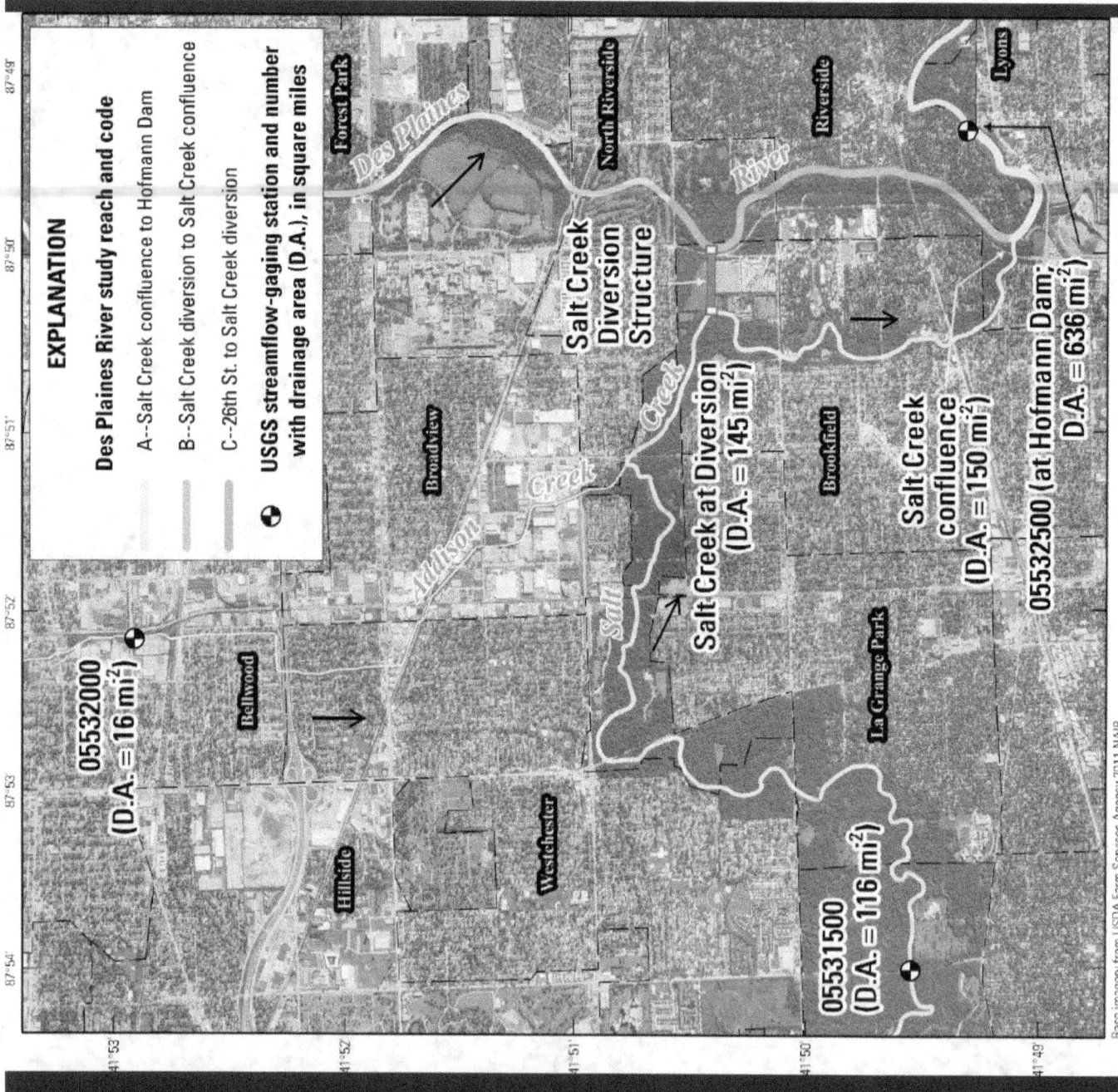

EXPLANATION

Des Plaines River study reach and code

A--Salt Creek confluence to Hofmann Dam

B--Salt Creek diversion to Salt Creek confluence

C--26th St. to Salt Creek diversion

● USGS streamflow-gaging station and number with drainage area (D.A.), in square miles

---

05532000 (D.A. = 16 mi²)

05531500 (D.A. = 116 mi²)

Salt Creek Diversion Structure

Salt Creek at Diversion (D.A. = 145 mi²)

Salt Creek confluence (D.A. = 150 mi²)

05532500 (at Hofmann Dam; D.A. = 636 mi²)

Forest Park

North Riverside

Riverside

Lyons

Broadview

Brookfield

La Grange Park

Bellwood

Hillside

Westchester

Des Plaines

River

Addison Creek

Salt Creek

→ Direction of flow

Base Imagery from USDA Farm Services Agency 2011 NAIP Natural Color Imagery for Illinois acquired between August 2, 2011 and September 15, 2011. Accessed in June 2012 at: http://gis.apfo.usda.gov/ArcGIS/services/NAIP/

1 MILE

1 KILOMETER

Beginning of complete water years (WY) of published daily streamflow record:

05531500: 10-1-1945
05532000: 10-1-1951
05532500: 10-1-1943

Note:
132 of 150 mi² (88%) of Salt Creek watershed is gaged.

Flow Data Computations

Reach C: Reach A flow – Salt Creek flow – Salt Creek diversion flow

Reach B: Reach A flow – Salt Creek flow

Reach A: Flow measurements from gage near Hofmann Dam

Des Plaines

Salt Creek Diversion Structure

River

Riverside

Salt Creek confluence (D.A. = 150 mi²)

05532500 (at Hofmann Dam; D.A. = 636 mi²)

Salt Creek Diversion Ratings

Notice major disagreement at low flows:

- OWR rating has 1 ft³/s diverted at 700 ft³/s in Salt Creek = 0.14% ~ 0.

- MWRD rating has 1280/2850 = 44.9% diverted up to 2850 ft³/s in Salt Creek.

- Our 5/17/12 measurement suggests low-flow rating is somewhere in the middle.

- Because of this uncertainty, flows based on both ratings were computed, providing a range of possible values.

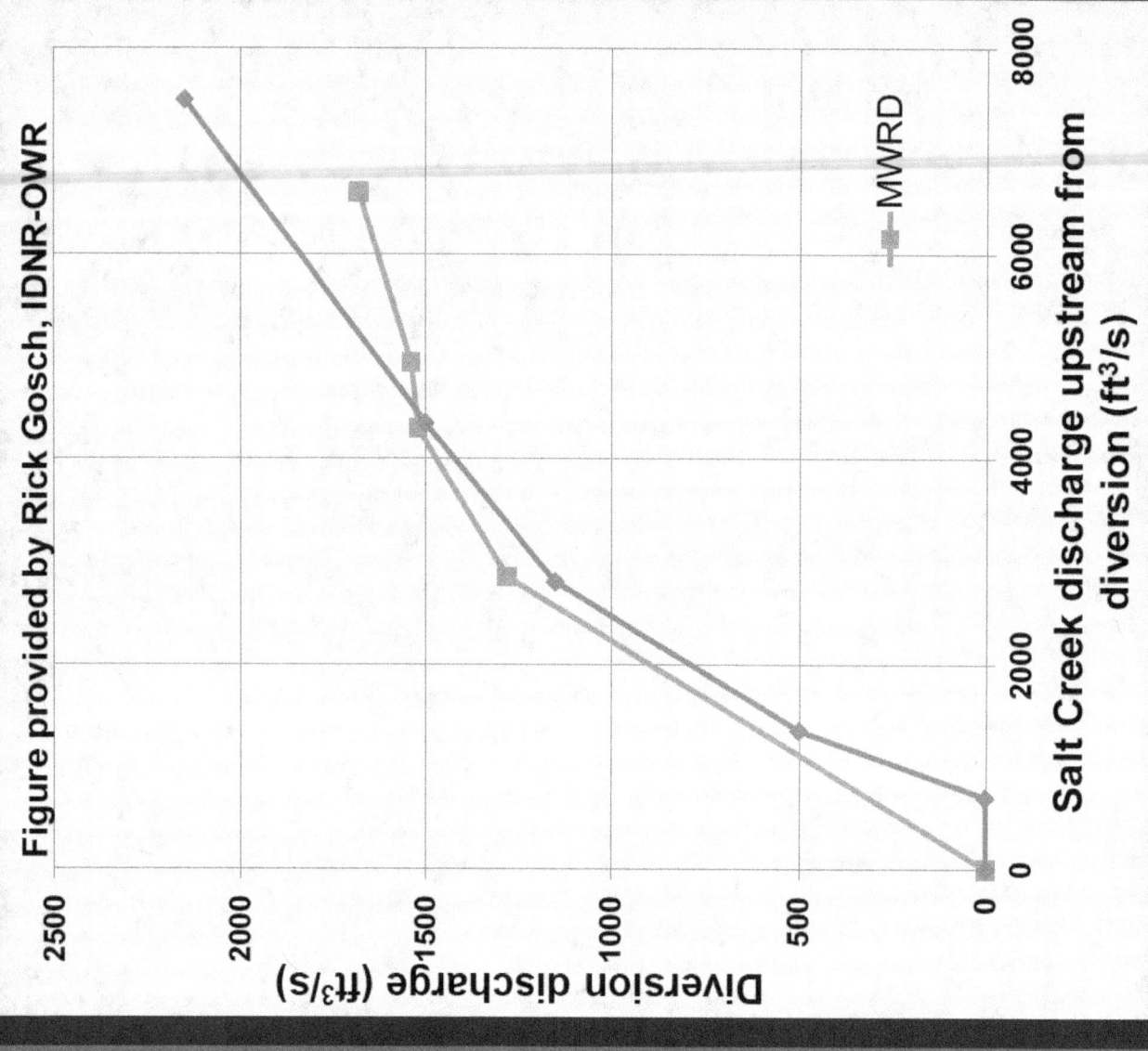

Figure provided by Rick Gosch, IDNR-OWR

Flow Data Computation: Uncertainties Considered

Rating of Salt Creek diversion affects flow computation for reach B

Adjustment for ungaged portion of Salt Creek at confluence affects flow computation for reaches B and C

Des Plaines

Salt Creek Diversion Structure

Riverside

River

Salt Creek confluence (D.A. = 150 mi²)

05532500 (at Hofmann Dam; D.A. = 636 mi²)

Trend Analysis of Annual Minimum 7-Day Flow (Q7), WY 1952–2010

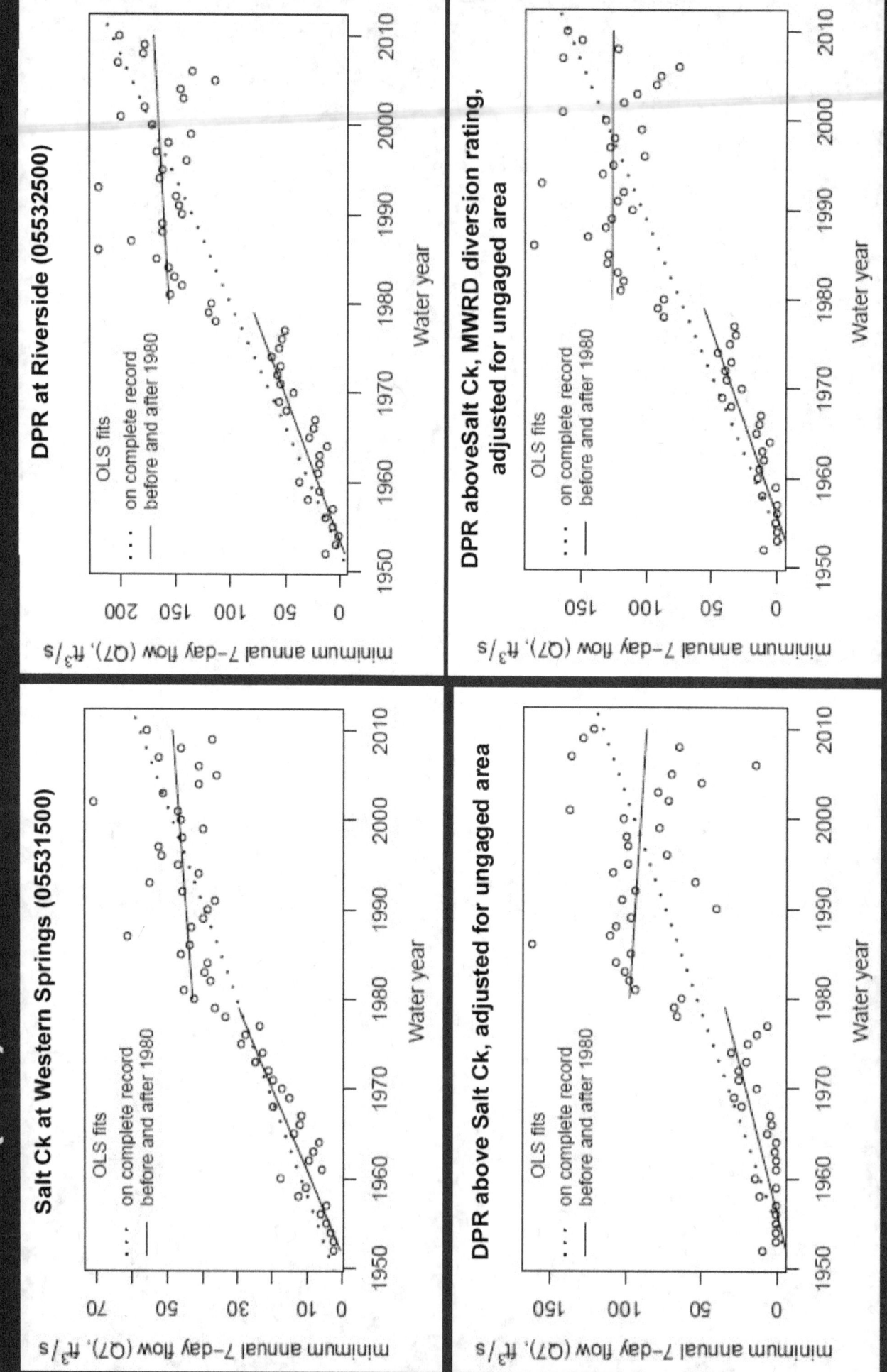

Trend Analysis of Annual Minimum 7-day Flow (Q7): Conclusions

- Trended upward in the 1950s and 1960s and then jumped during the mid-to-late 1970s

- Trends since 1980 are small and not statistically different than zero

➤ Estimate 7Q10 from 1980–2010 Q7 data

USGS

7Q10 Computation Results (ft³/s)

Reach C: [47.3 – 62.0] (88*)

Reach B: [47.3 – 101] (90*)

Reach A: 131 (133*)

*Values in italics are from the Illinois State Water Survey (2003), included for comparison.

Trend Analysis of Annual Quantiles of 80% Exceedance Daily Flow ($Q_{0.80}$)

Salt Ck at Western Springs (05531500)

DPR at Riverside (05532500)

DPR above Salt Ck, adjusted for ungaged area

DPR above Salt Ck, MWRD diversion rating, adjusted for ungaged area

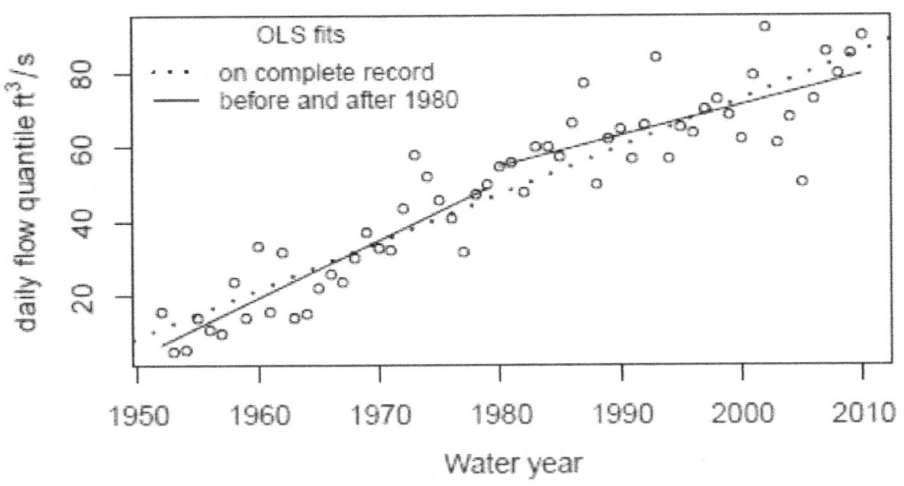

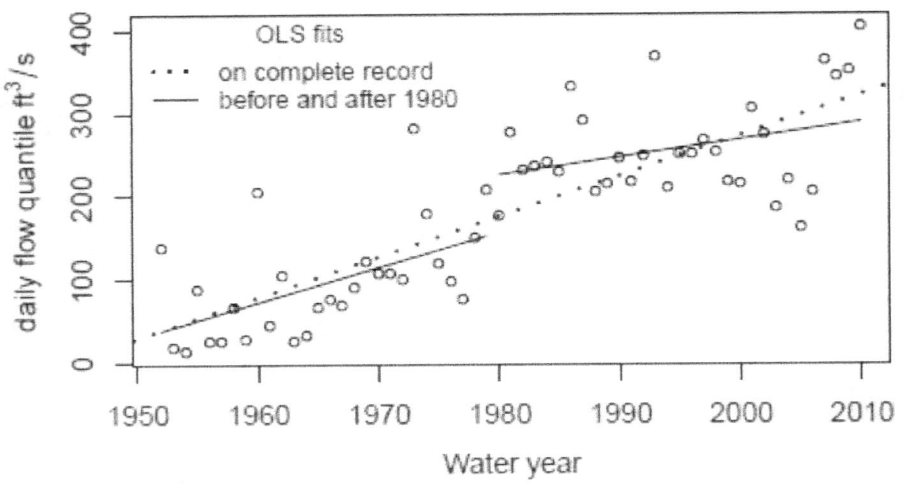

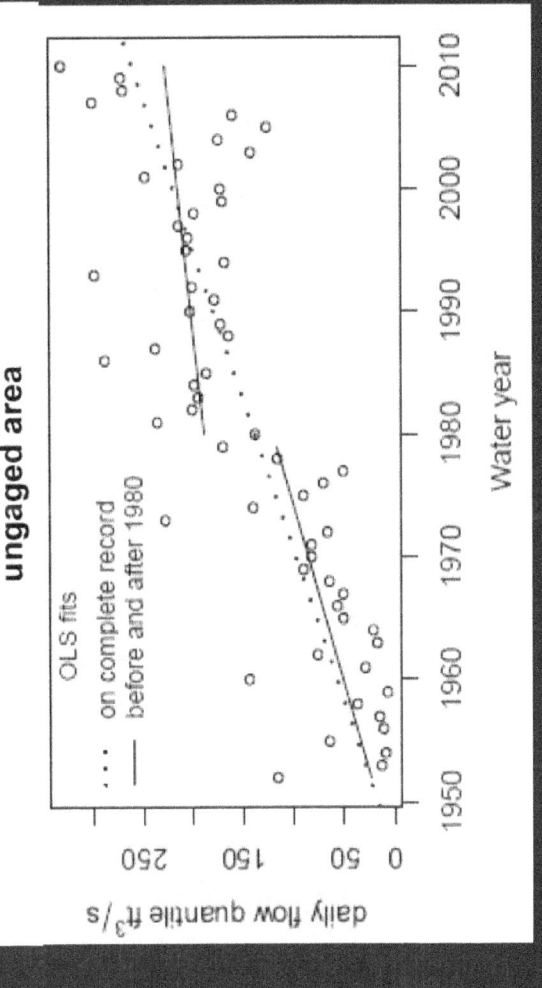

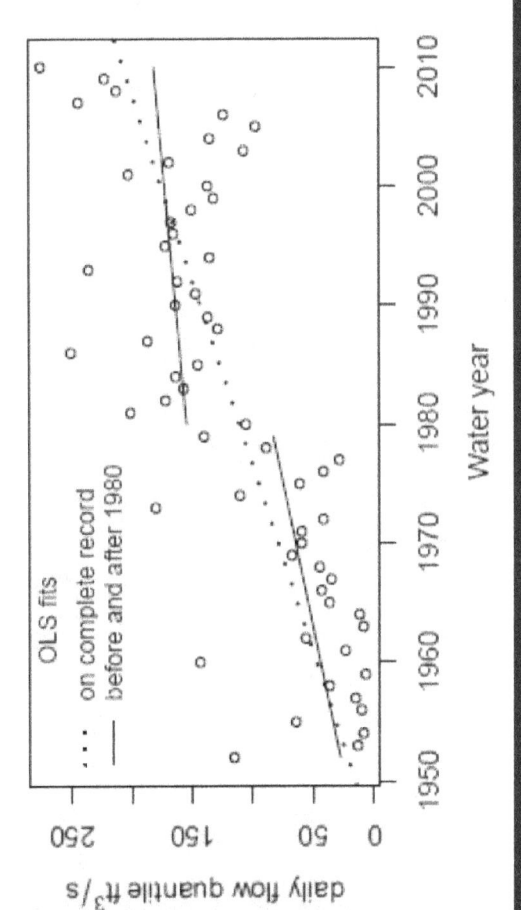

Trend Analysis of Daily Flow Flow Quantiles: Conclusions

- Trends in quantiles of interest are generally positive throughout the period of record (1952–2010).

- As with the Q7 data, there is a break in the trend in mid-to-late 1970s.

- Unlike the Q7 data, trends since 1980 are positive.

- Use data from 2000–2010[1] to compute daily flow quantiles.

[1]This time period is a compromise between being recent and having enough data to estimate the flow value with reasonable accuracy.

≋USGS

80% Exceedance Daily Flow Computation Results (ft³/s)

Reach C: [149 – 160] (161*)

Reach B: [149 – 199] (161*)

Reach A: 245 (246*)

*Values in italics are from OWR presentation, Sept. 2011.

Hydraulic Model Results

Water-surface elevations were modeled using:

- Manning's roughness of 0.035
- USGS computed flows (no diversion and diversion added)

Results are presented as:

- Longitudinal profiles (80% exceedance and 7Q10)
- Cross section views (7Q10)
- Tables (80% exceedance and 7Q10)

≈USGS

Conditions Modeled

- ## Hofmann Dam current conditions

  - - - - - - Existing (no diversion)
  - - - ■ - - Existing (diversion added)

- ## 150-ft notch in Hofmann Dam

  ———— Proposed (no diversion)
  ——■—— Proposed (diversion added)

≋USGS

Hydraulic Model Result Locations

— 26th to 31st Street

— 31st to Railroad Bridge

— Railroad Bridge to Salt Creek

— Salt Creek to Hofmann Dam

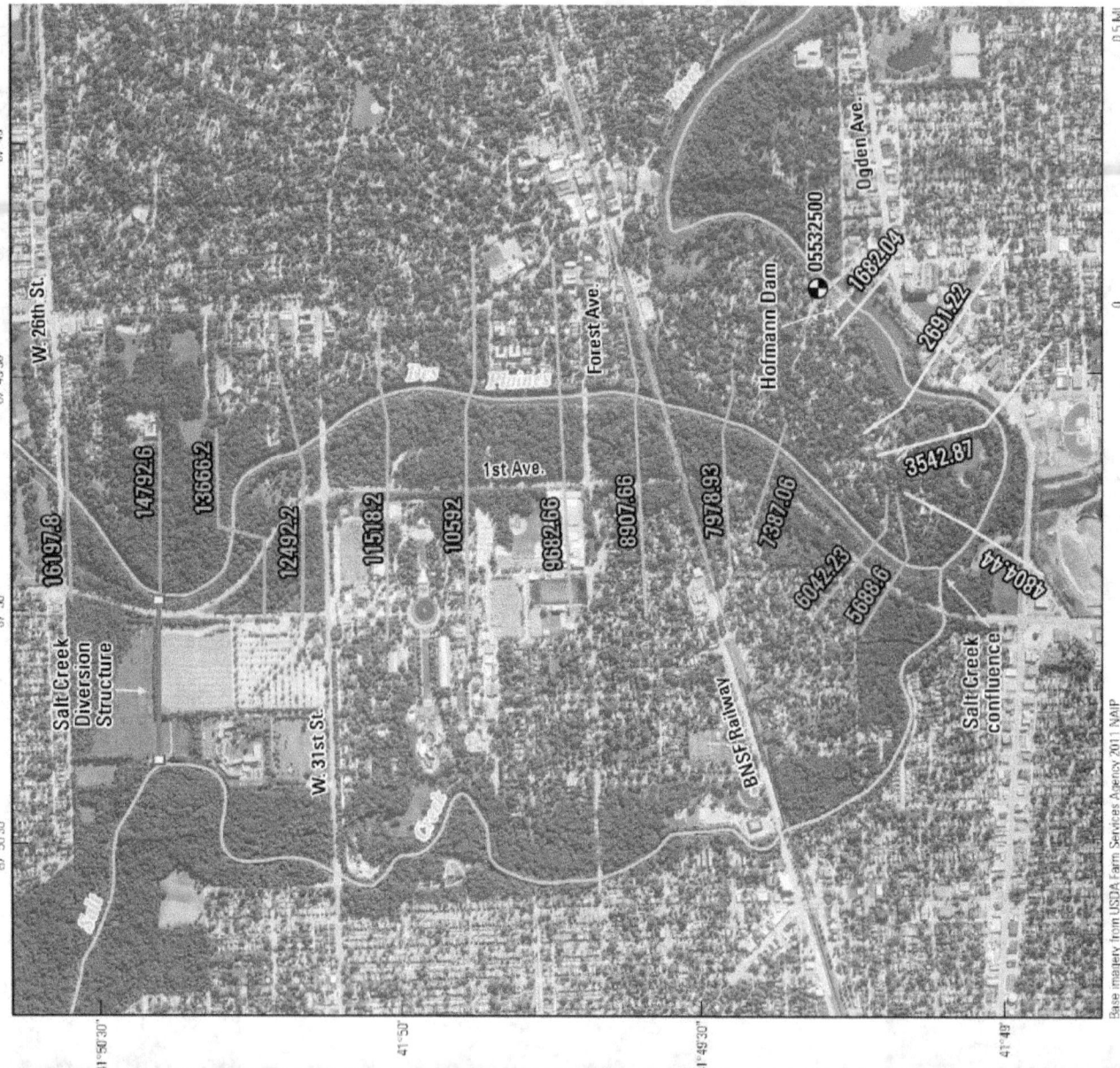

EXPLANATION

⊕ USGS streamflow-gaging station and number

1682.04 ——— Synoptic cross section with river station label

Base imagery from USDA Farm Services Agency 2011 NAIP
Natural Color Imagery for Illinois acquired between August 2, 2011
and September 15, 2011. Accessed in June 2012 at
http://gis.apfo.usda.gov/ArcGIS/services/NAIP/

≋USGS

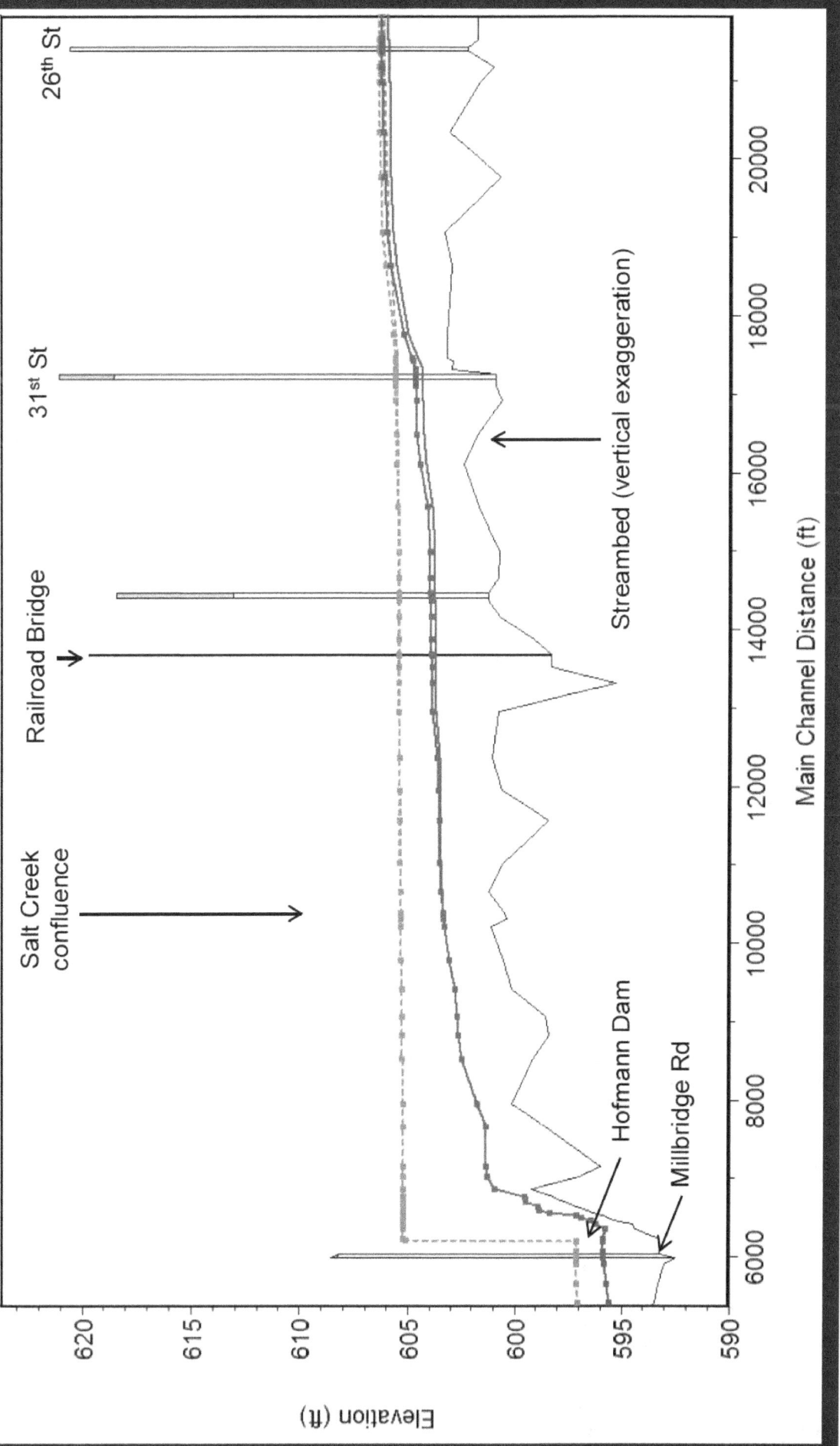

Longitudinal Profile
80% Exceedance

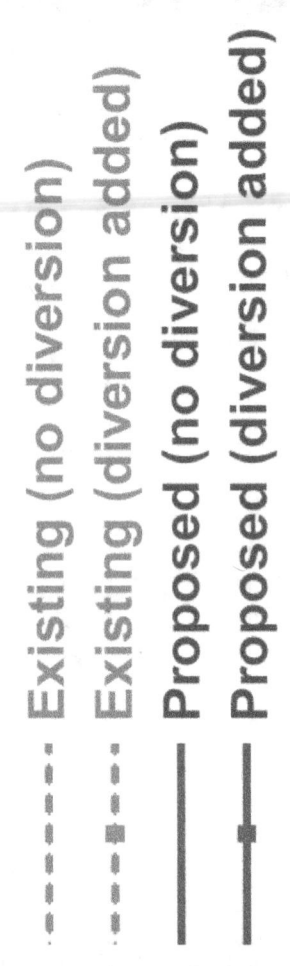

Longitudinal Profile
80% Exceedance

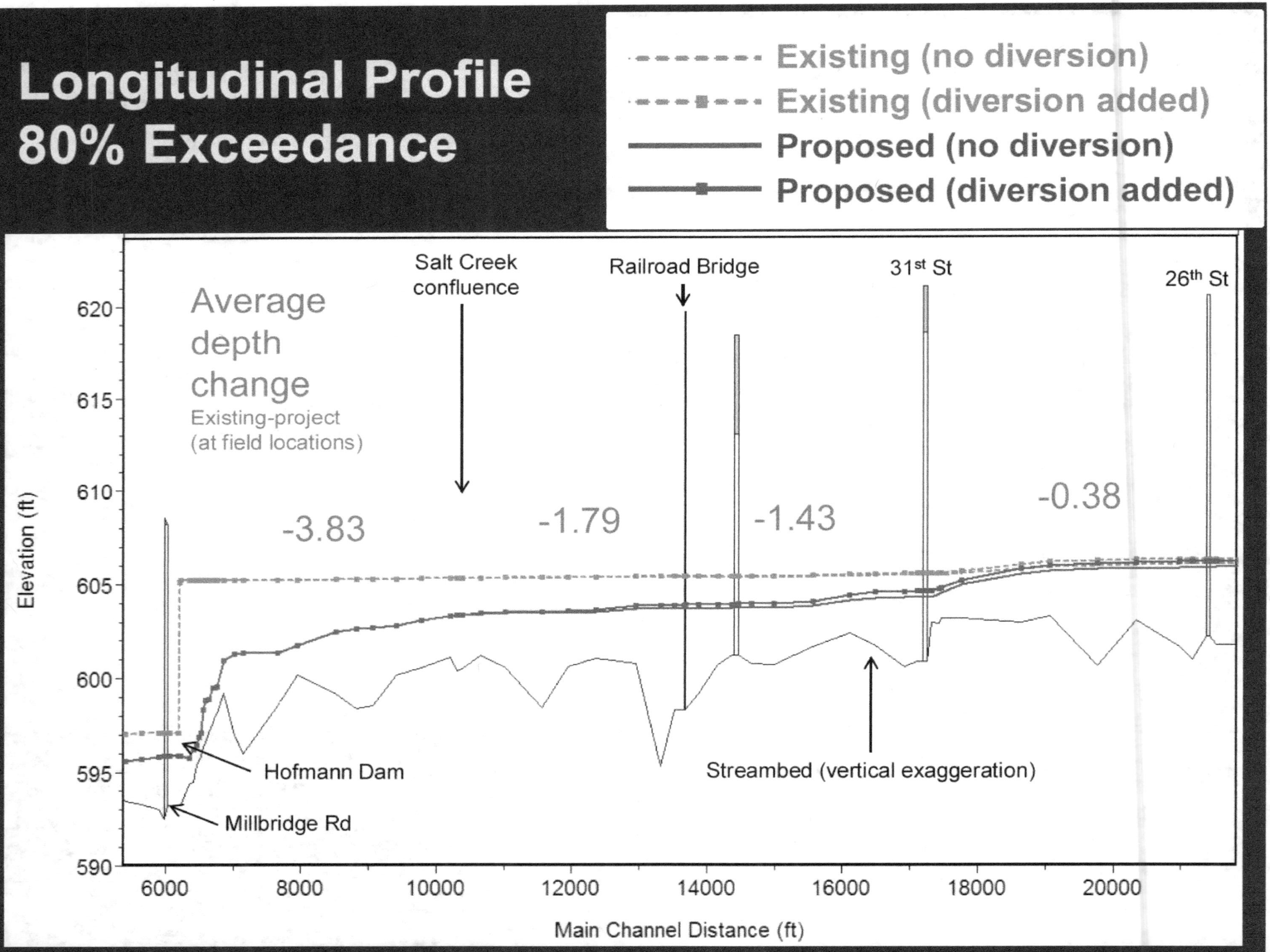

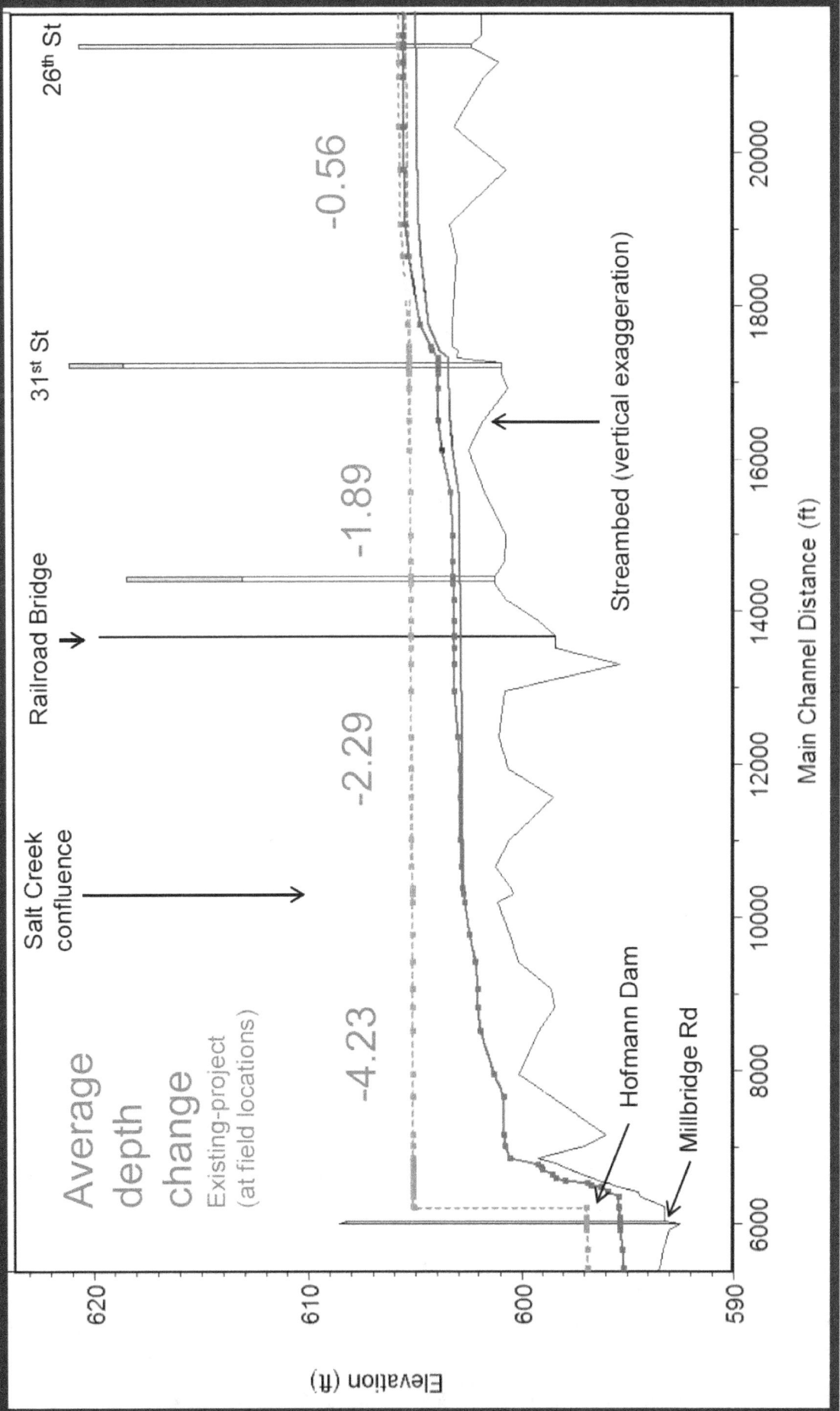

Longitudinal Profile 7Q10

Hydraulic Model Result Locations

— 26th to 31st Street

— 31st to Railroad Bridge

— Railroad Bridge to Salt Creek

— Salt Creek to Hofmann Dam

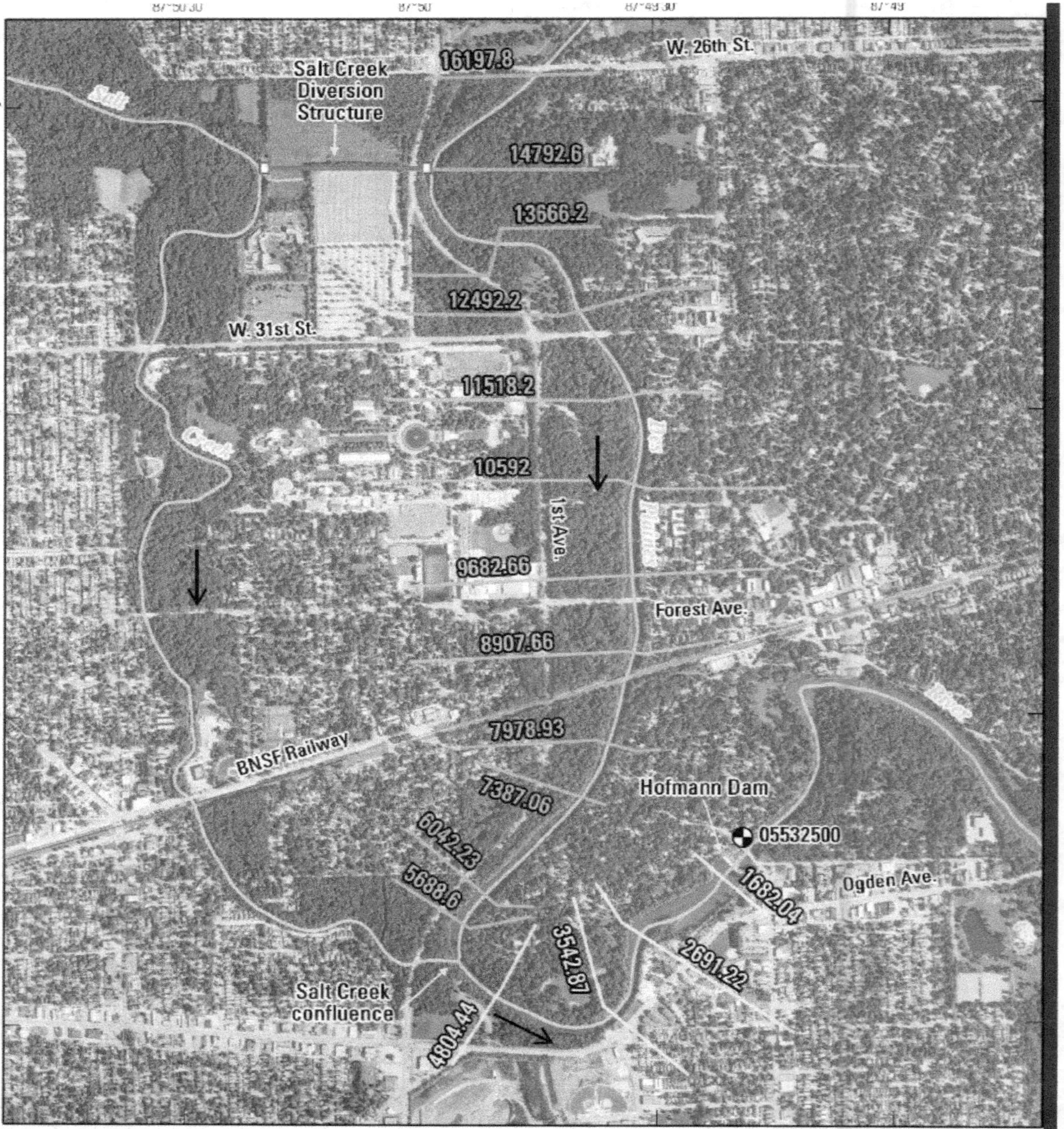

EXPLANATION

⬤ USGS streamflow-gaging station and number

—— Synoptic cross section with river station label

1682.04

→ Direction of flow

0   0.5 MILE

0   0.5 KILOMETER

Base imagery from USDA Farm Services Agency 2011 NAIP
Natural Color Imagery for Illinois acquired between August 2, 2011
and September 15, 2011. Accessed in June 2012 at
http://gis.apfo.usda.gov/ArcGIS/services/NAIP/

Map labels:

W. 26th St.

W. 31st St.

Des Plaines

Forest Ave.

1st Ave.

Ogden Ave.

Salt Creek Diversion Structure

Hofmann Dam

BNSF Railway

Salt Creek confluence

05532500

16197.8
14792.6
13566.2
12492.2
11518.2
10592
9682.66
8907.66
7978.93
7387.06
6042.23
5688.6
4804.44
3542.87
2691.22
1682.04

41°50'30"
41°50'
41°49'30"
41°49'

Example Cross Section Plot and Line Legend

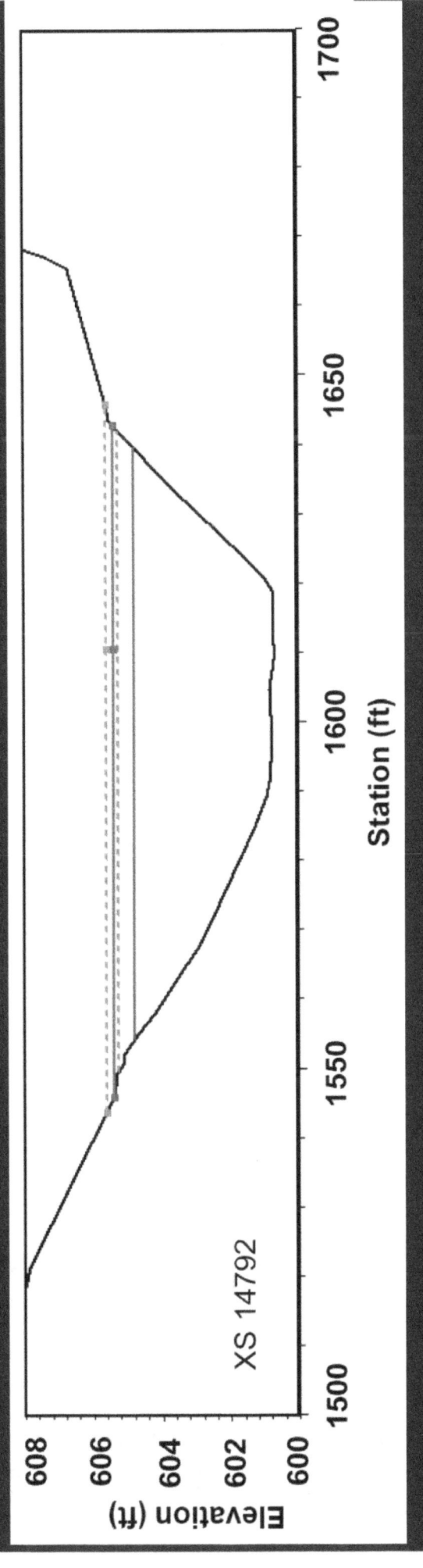

Existing (no diversion)
Existing (diversion added)
Proposed (no diversion)
Proposed (diversion added)

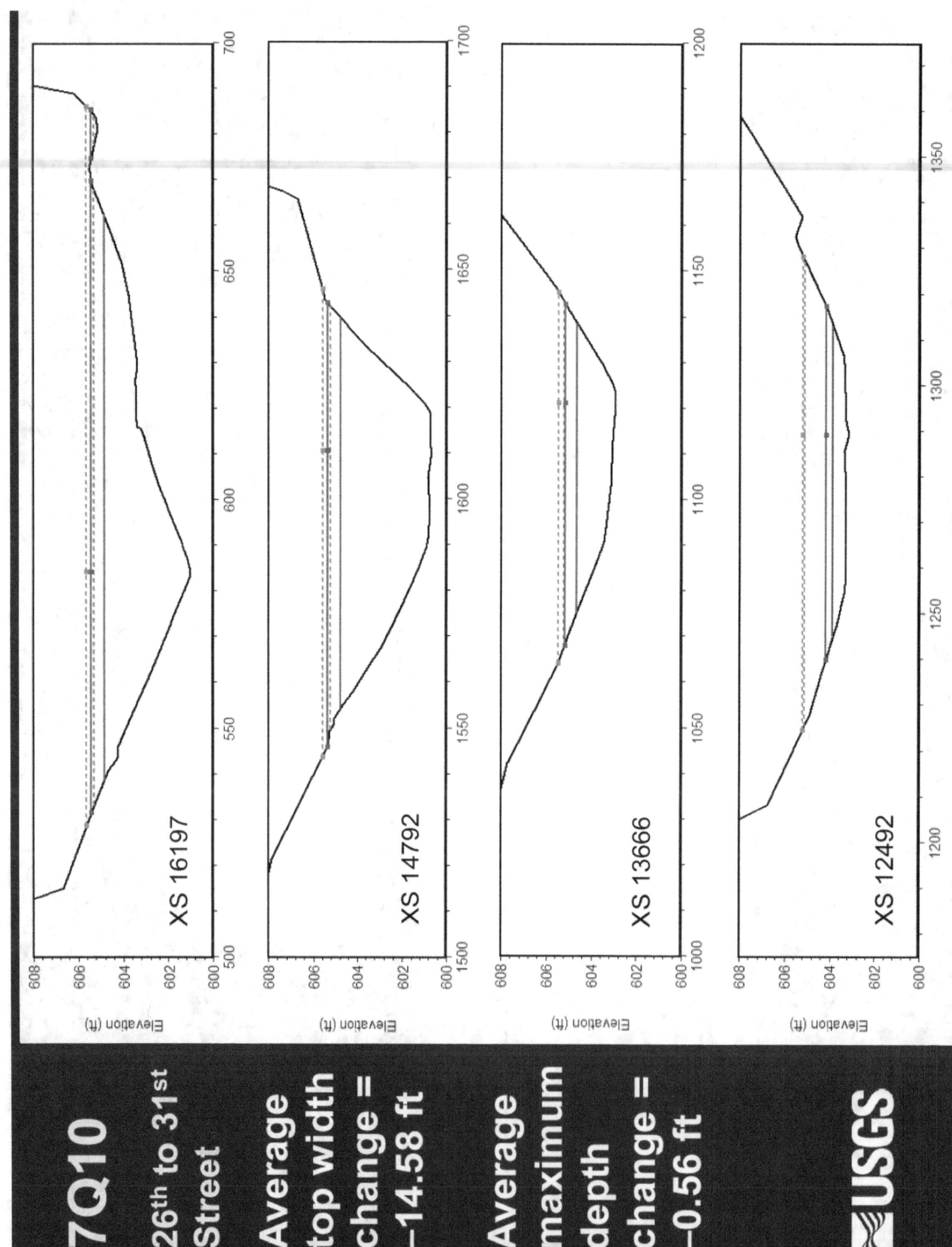

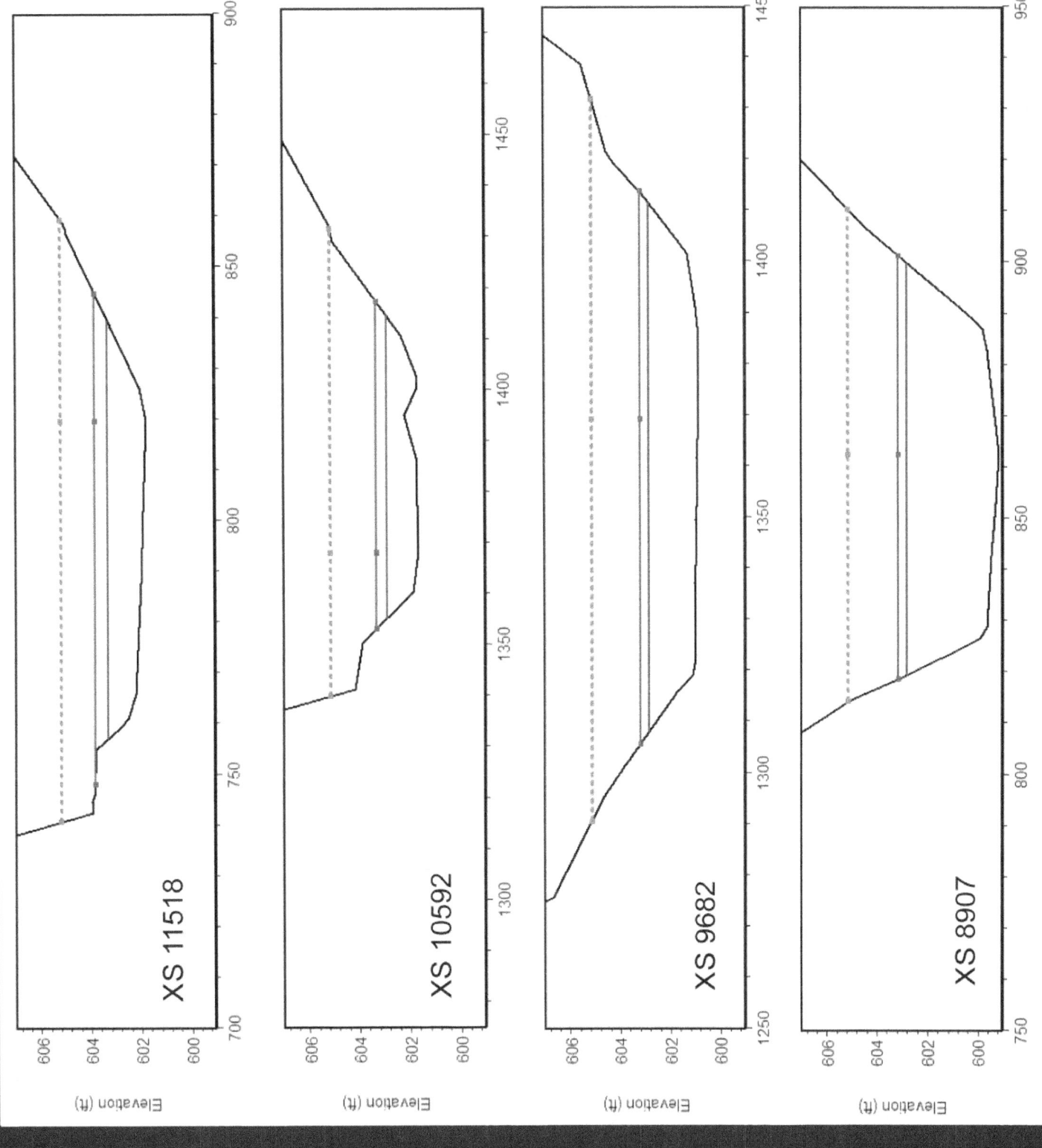

7Q10

31st Street to Railroad Bridge

Average top width change = −27.04 ft

Average maximum depth change = −1.98 ft

USGS

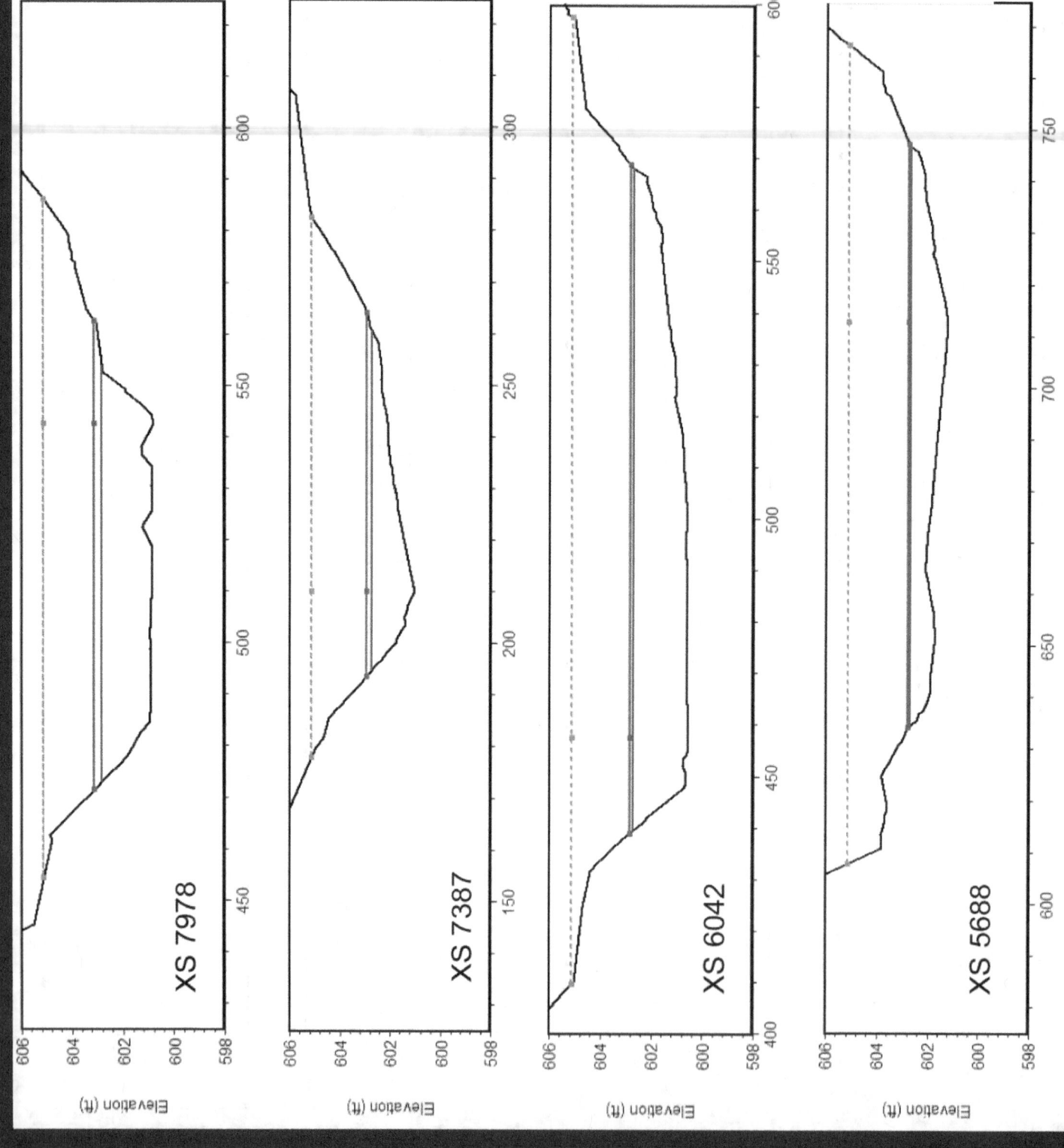

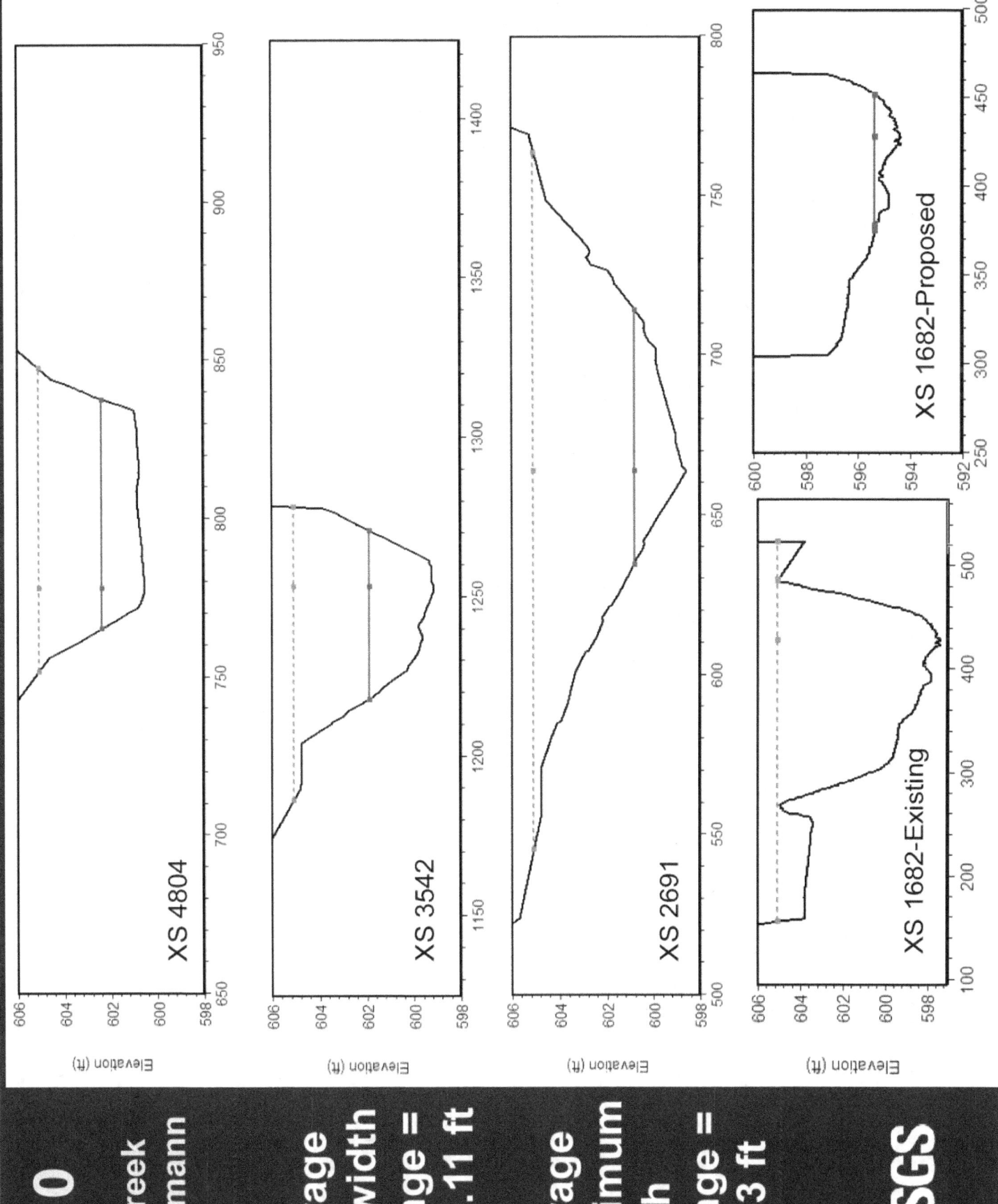

Summary of USGS Activities

Summary of Field Data Collection

- Data collected for model verification

- Flow measurements collected for model verification

- Water-surface elevations collected for model verification

- Field-estimated Manning's roughness ranged from 0.035 to 0.045

- Observed flow in Salt Creek diversion consistent with measured value

USGS

Summary of Model Verification

- Hydraulic model verified from 31st Street to Hofmann Dam
  - Observed to modeled error +/– 0.16 ft (for 0.035 Manning's roughness model)
- Manning's roughness of 0.035 selected
  - The USACE model value was 0.040 (error +/– 0.21 ft)
  - Both values are within range of field estimations

USGS

Summary of Hydrologic Analysis

- Analysis of annual flow statistics indicated:
  - Increasing flows in all statistics throughout 1950s–70s
  - Use of flow data from 1980–2010 for annual 7-day minimum and 2000–10 for 20%, 50%, and 80% exceedance daily flow quantiles
- Range of flow statistic values estimated for reaches above Salt Creek confluence depending on:
  - diversion rating
  - Salt Creek unmeasured drainage area

USGS

Summary of Hydraulic Analysis: Change in Top Width

- 16 cross sections total (four in each reach)

Reach Location	7Q10 Flows (project minus existing) Average Top Width Change (ft)	80th Percentile Flows (project minus existing) Average Top Width Change (ft)
31st Street to 26th Street	-14.58	-9.86
Railroad to 31st Street	-27.04	-19.00
Salt Creek to Railroad	-46.57	-39.30
Hofmann Dam to Salt Creek	-123.11	-116.09

USGS

Summary of Hydraulic Analysis: Change in Maximum Depth

- 16 cross sections total (four in each reach)

Reach Location	7Q10 Flows (project minus existing) Average Maximum Depth Change (ft)	80th Percentile Flows (project minus existing) Average Maximum Depth Change (ft)
31st Street to 26th Street	-0.56	-0.38
Railroad to 31st Street	-1.98	-1.43
Salt Creek to Railroad	-2.29	-1.79
Hofmann Dam to Salt Creek	-4.23	-3.83

USGS

Hydrologic Analysis:
Additional Methods and Results Slides

- Specific details on the methods and results of the hydrologic and hydraulic analyses are presented in the following slides including:

  - Detailed information on hydrologic analysis methods and specific results for the 50 and 20 percentiles

  - Detailed summary tables of all model results for the 80%, 50%, and 20% exceedance daily flow quantiles and 7Q10 flow statistics

Wastewater Treatment Plant Effluent Flows

Table 2.2: Inflows above Station 05531500: Salt Creek at Western Springs

Source	Inflows (cfs)						
	1940	1950	1960	1970	1980	1990	
John Egan Plant	-	-	-	-	19.5	24.6	
Elk Grove Devon	-	-	-	-	0.1	-	
Springbrook	-	0.03	0.42	0.80	1.5	3.4	
Wood Dale	-	-	0.36	1.1	1.7	2.0	
Addison	0.08	0.08	0.88	3.8	5.5	5.9	
Salt Creek S. D.	1.1	1.4	3.4	4.6	2.8	2.0	
Elmhurst	1.9	2.6	4.8	7.3	10.4	6.5	
Oakbrook Terrace	-	-	-	0.12	-	-	
Oak Brook	-	-	0.09	1.6	-	-	
Total	3.08	4.11	9.95	19.32	41.5	44.4	

Table from Singh and Ramamurthy (1993)

Also note online information indicates MWRD Kirie WWTP, which discharges to Willow Creek. Kirie WWTP discharge enters the Des Plaines River below USGS streamflow-gaging station 0552900 but above the study area and began operation in 1980.

≋USGS

ISWS 7Q10 Maps

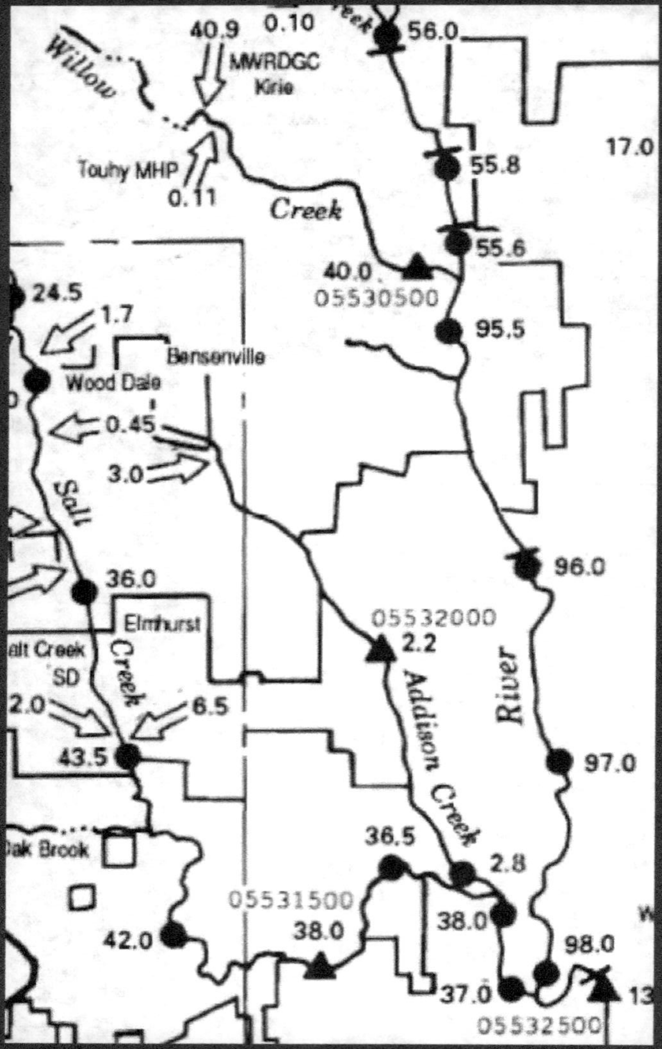

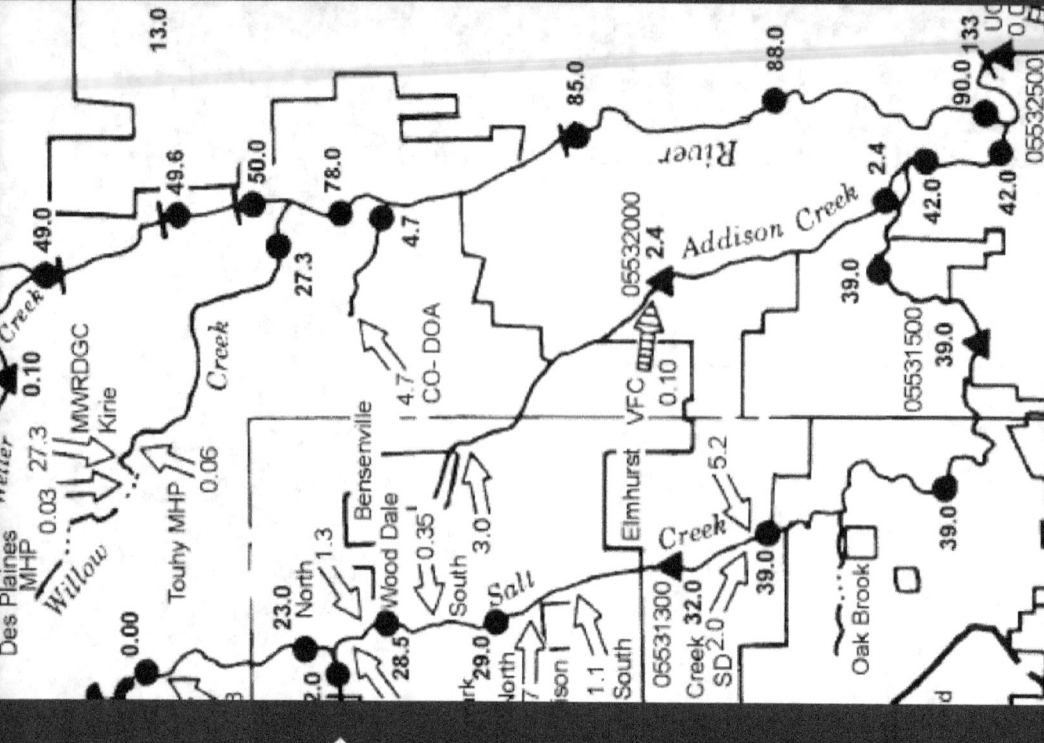

← 1993
2003 →

Notes:
- Channel losses in Lower Salt Creek in 1993 map but not 2003.
- Decrease in Kirie WWTP flows from 1993 to 2003, which explain part but not all of Des Plaines River decreases from 1993 to 2003.

 USGS

Flow Data Sources and Computation Methods: Des Plaines River

Location	Data Source or Computation Method
Reach A: DPR below Salt Ck confluence	$Q_{DPR.Riverside}$
Reach B: DPR above Salt Ck confluence / below Salt Ck diversion	$Q_{DPR.abvSalt.MWRDdiv} = Q_{DPR.Riverside} - Q_{SaltCk.conf}$
Reach C: DPR above Salt Ck diversion	$Q_{DPR.abvSalt} = Q_{DPR.Riverside} - Q_{SaltCk.conf} - Q_{div}$

Notes:
- Stylized Q indicates estimated quantity; others are measured.
- $Q_{DPR.Riverside}$: daily streamflow at USGS streamgage 05532500.
- $Q_{SaltCk.conf}$: daily streamflow at Salt Creek confluence with DPR
- Q_{div}: daily streamflow in Salt Creek diversion

Flow Data Sources and Computation Methods: Salt Creek

Location	Data Source or Computation Method
Salt Creek at confluence	$Q_{SaltCk.conf} = K_{DA.adj.conf}[Q_{SaltCk.WSprings} + Q_{AddisonCk}] - Q_{div}$, where $K_{DA.adj.conf} = DA_{SaltCk.conf}/(DA_{SaltCkWSprings} + DA_{AddisonCk}) =$ $150.4/(116.3+16.2) = 1.135$; $K_{DA.adj.conf} = 1$ for no ungaged area adjustment.
Salt Creek diversion	$Q_{div} = K_{rating} {}^* Q_{SaltCk.at.div}$ $K_{rating} = 0.449$ (MWRD) or 0.0 (IDNR-OWR)
Salt Creek at diversion	$Q_{SaltCk.at.div} = K_{DA.adj.div}[Q_{SaltCk.WSprings} + Q_{AddisonCk}]$, where $K_{DA.adj.div} = DA_{SaltCk.at.div}/(DA_{SaltCkWSprings} + DA_{AddisonCk}) =$ $145.3/(116.3+16.2) = 1.0966$; $K_{DA.adj.div} = 1$ for no ungaged area adjustment.

Notes:
- Stylized Q indicates estimated quantity; others are measured.
- $Q_{AddisonCk}$: daily streamflow at USGS streamgage 05532000.
- $Q_{SaltCk.WSprings}$: daily streamflow at USGS streamgage 05531500.
- DA: drainage areas in square miles from USGS StreamStats.

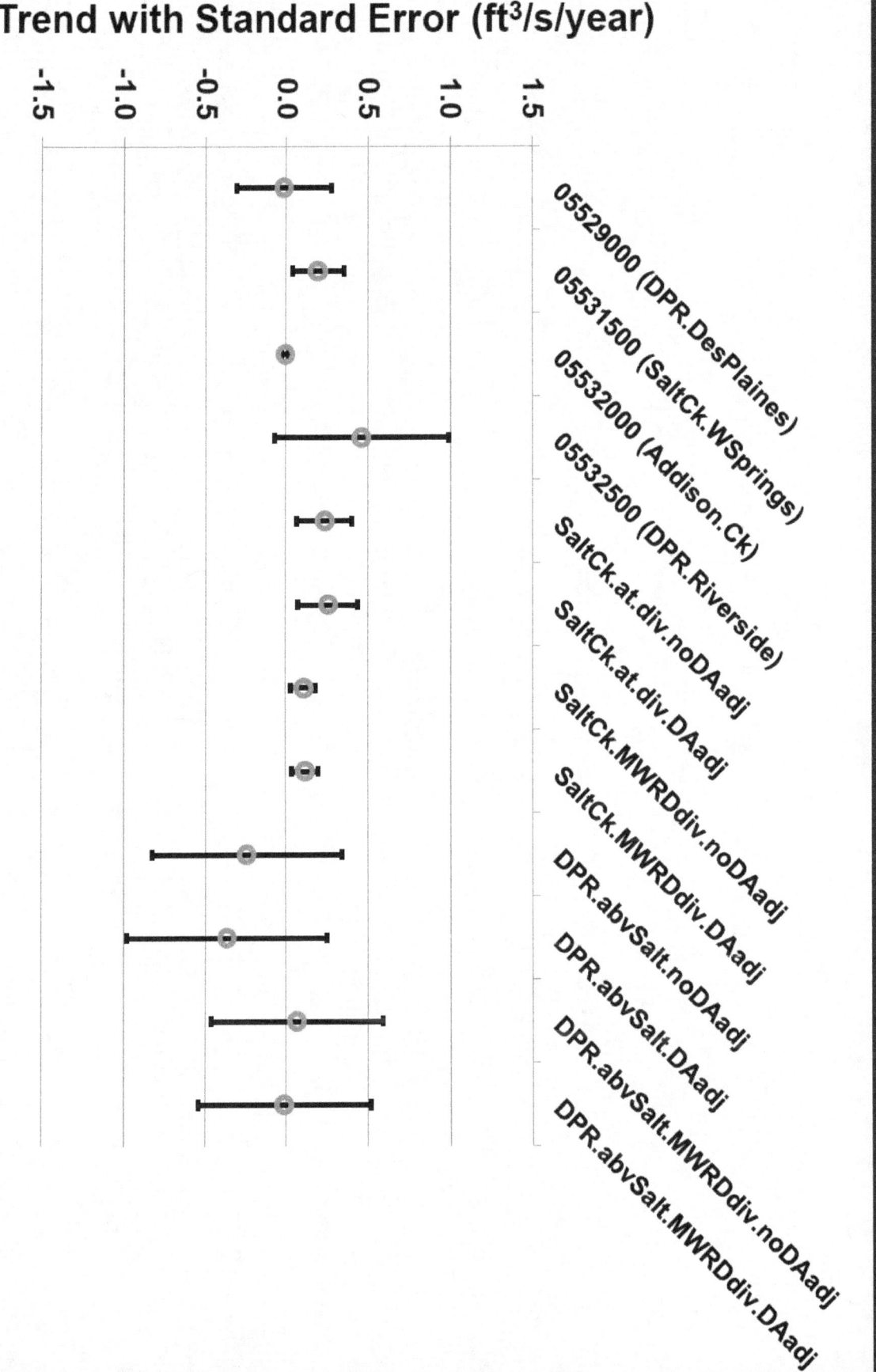

Computation of 7Q10:
log-Pearson type 3 (LP3) Method

- Determine a homogeneous period (here 1980–2010)

- Compute moments (mean, stdev, skewness) of $\log_{10}$ of annual minimum 7-day flow ($\log_{10}$Q7) series

- Fit to "Pearson type 3" distribution using moments to constrain parameters (in this study function *quape3()* from version 1.6.1 of *lmomco* package (Asquith, 2012) of *R* language was used for this fit).

- Note: Flood frequency computations are usually done essentially the same way (Interagency Advisory Committee on Water Data, 1981).

≈USGS

Computation of 7Q10: Example Fits

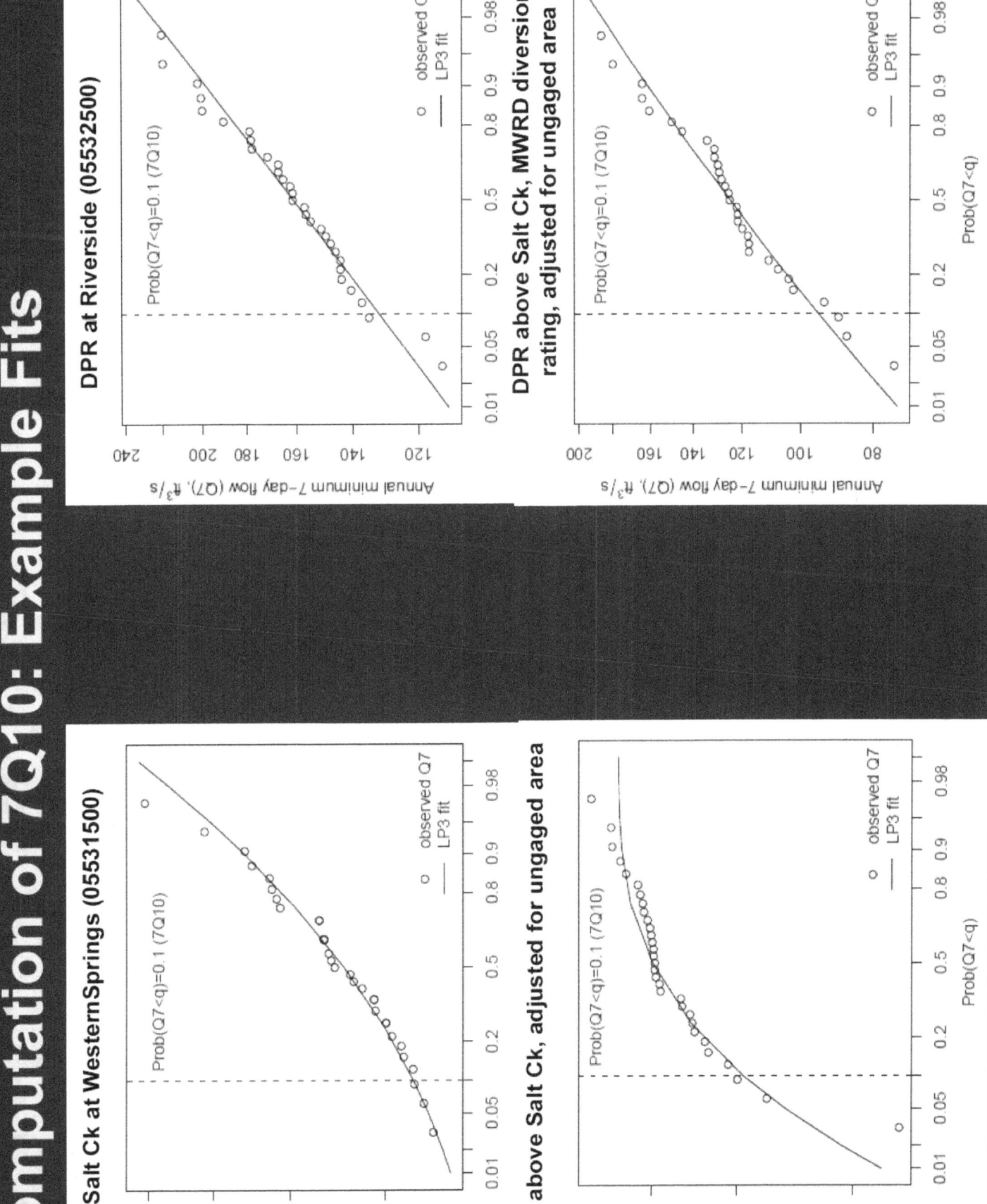

Computation of 7Q10: Results

Applicable Des Plaines River reach	Drainage area adjustment	Salt Creek diversion included	Estimated 7Q10: this study (ft³/s)	Estimated 7Q10: ISWS 2003 (ft³/s)
Reach A: below Salt Ck	N/A	N/A	131	133
	No	Yes	101	90
Reach B: above Salt Ck, below diversion	Yes	Yes	94.5	90
	No	No	62.0	90
	Yes	No	47.3	90
Reach C: above Salt Ck, above diversion	No	N/A	62.0	88
	Yes	N/A	47.3	88

Daily Flow Quantiles: Computation Example

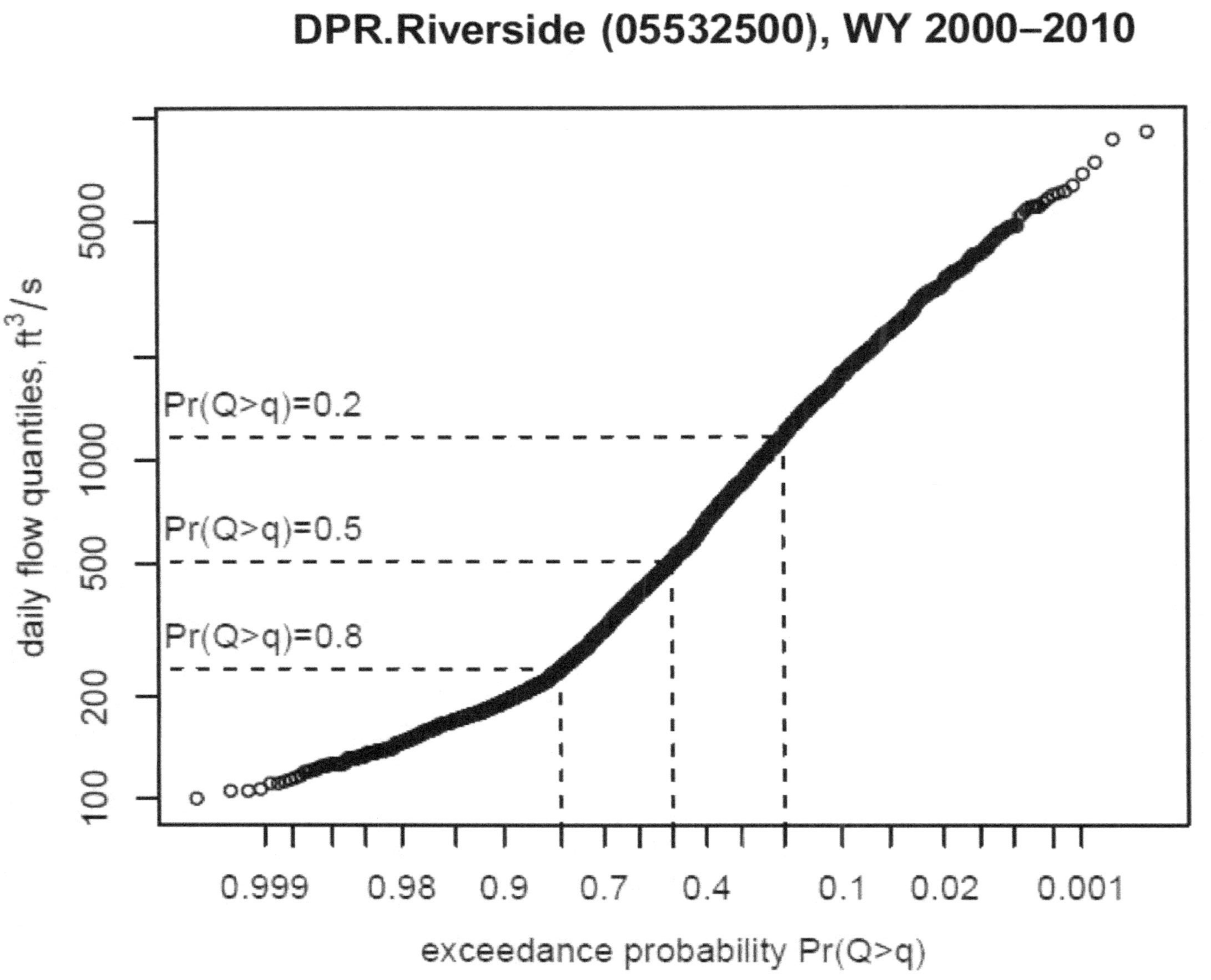

USGS

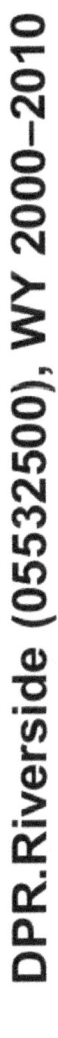

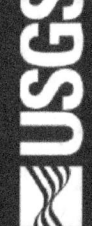

Trend Analysis of Daily Flow Quantiles Method

- Example computation plot in previous slide used 11 years of data.

- To analyze trends, daily flow quantiles were obtained from each water year's data separately to obtain quantiles on an annual basis.

- Example results of trend analysis of these annual quantiles for 50% and 20% exceedance probabilities are given in the following slides; 80% exceedance results were given in main body of presentation.

USGS

Trend Analysis: Annual Quantiles of 50% Exceedance Daily Flow

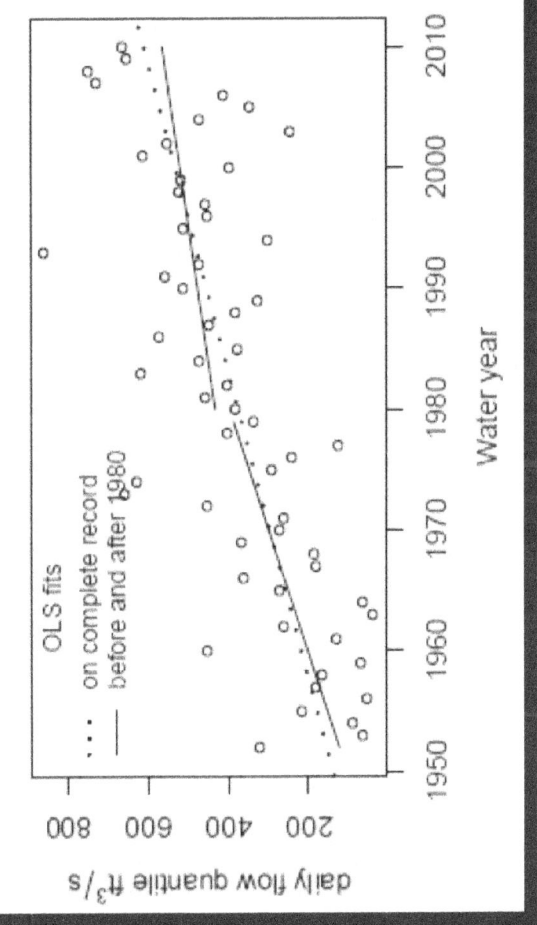

DPR at Riverside (05532500)

OLS fits
- ··· on complete record
- —— before and after 1980

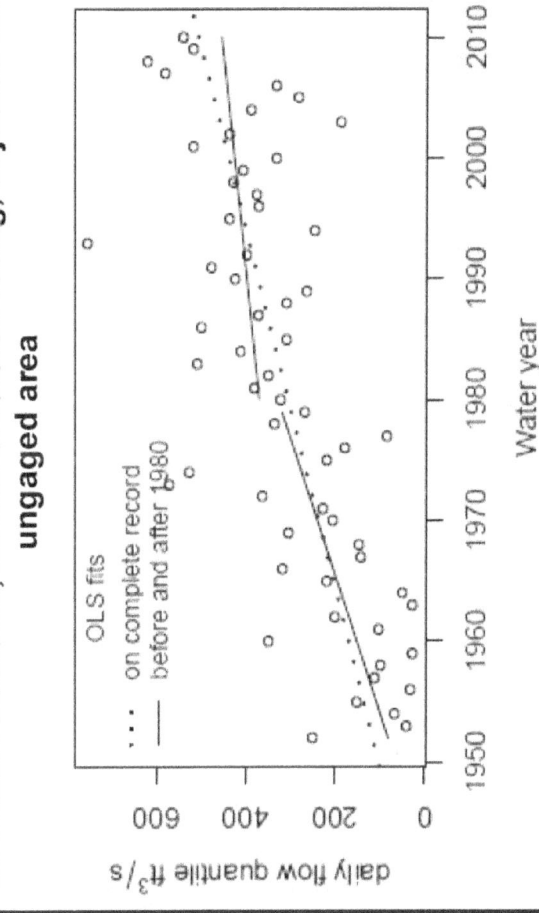

DPR above Salt Ck, MWRD diversion rating, adjusted for ungaged area

OLS fits
- ··· on complete record
- —— before and after 1980

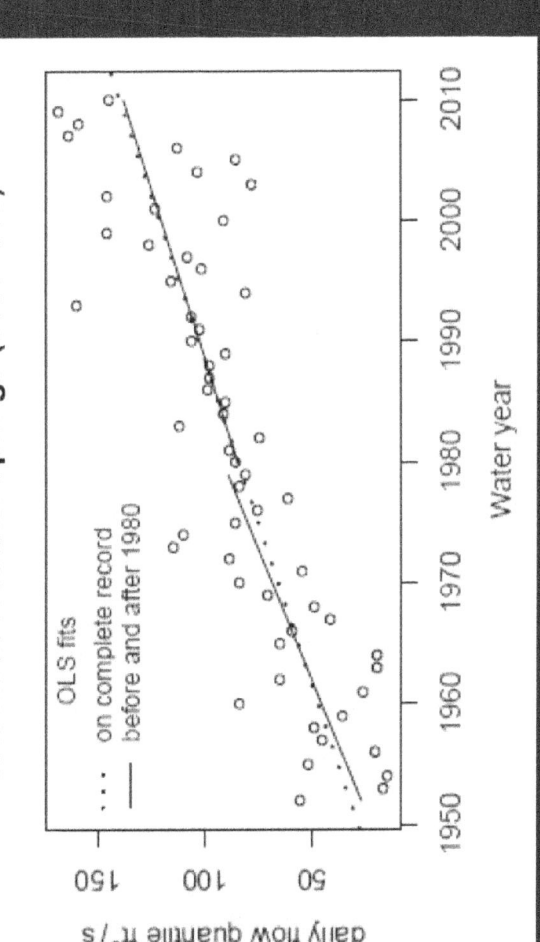

Salt Ck at Western Springs (05531500)

OLS fits
- ··· on complete record
- —— before and after 1980

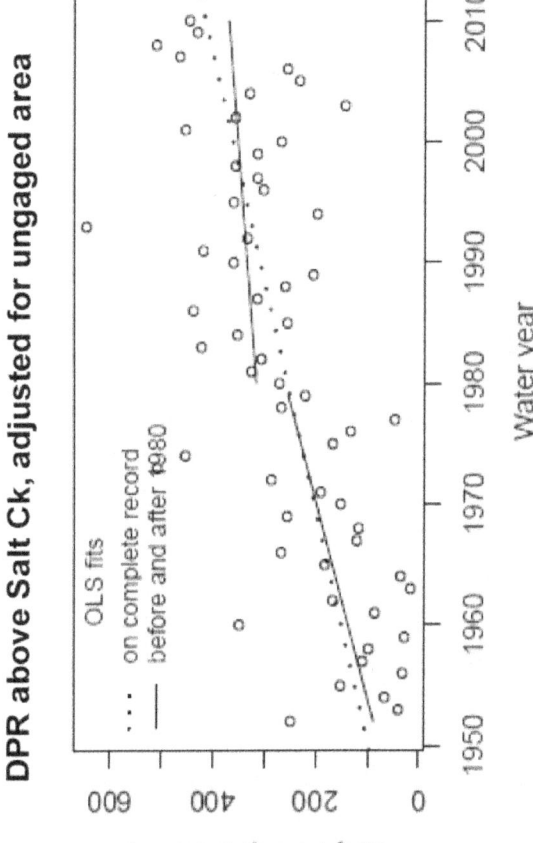

DPR above Salt Ck, adjusted for ungaged area

OLS fits
- ··· on complete record
- —— before and after 1980

Trend Analysis: Annual Quantiles of 20% Exceedance Daily Flow

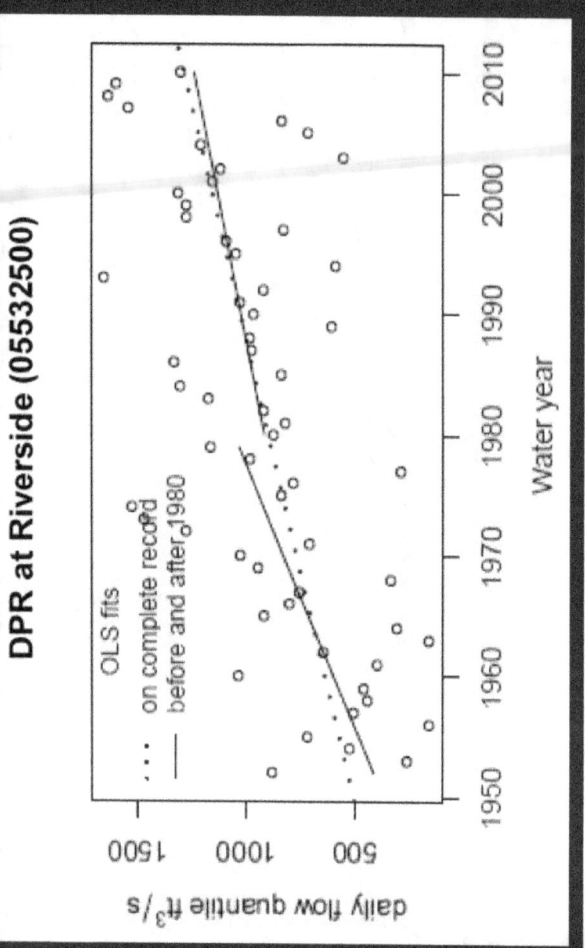

Salt Ck at Western Springs (05531500)

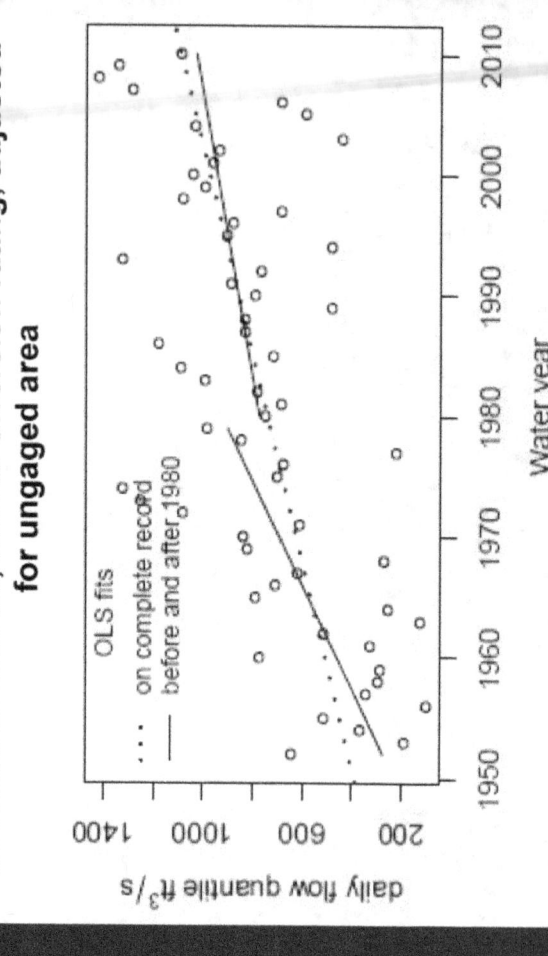

DPR at Riverside (05532500)

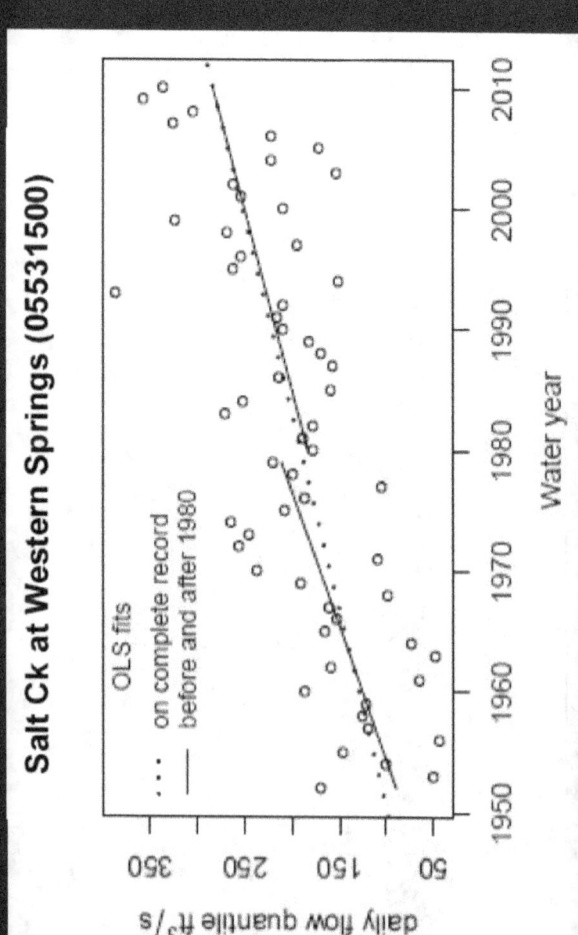

DPR above Salt Ck, adjusted for ungaged area

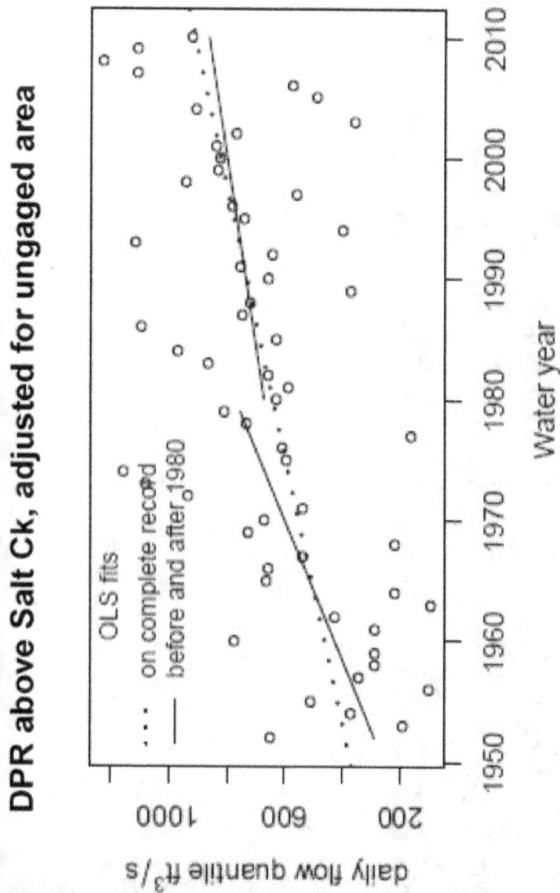

DPR above Salt Ck, MWRD diversion rating, adjusted for ungaged area

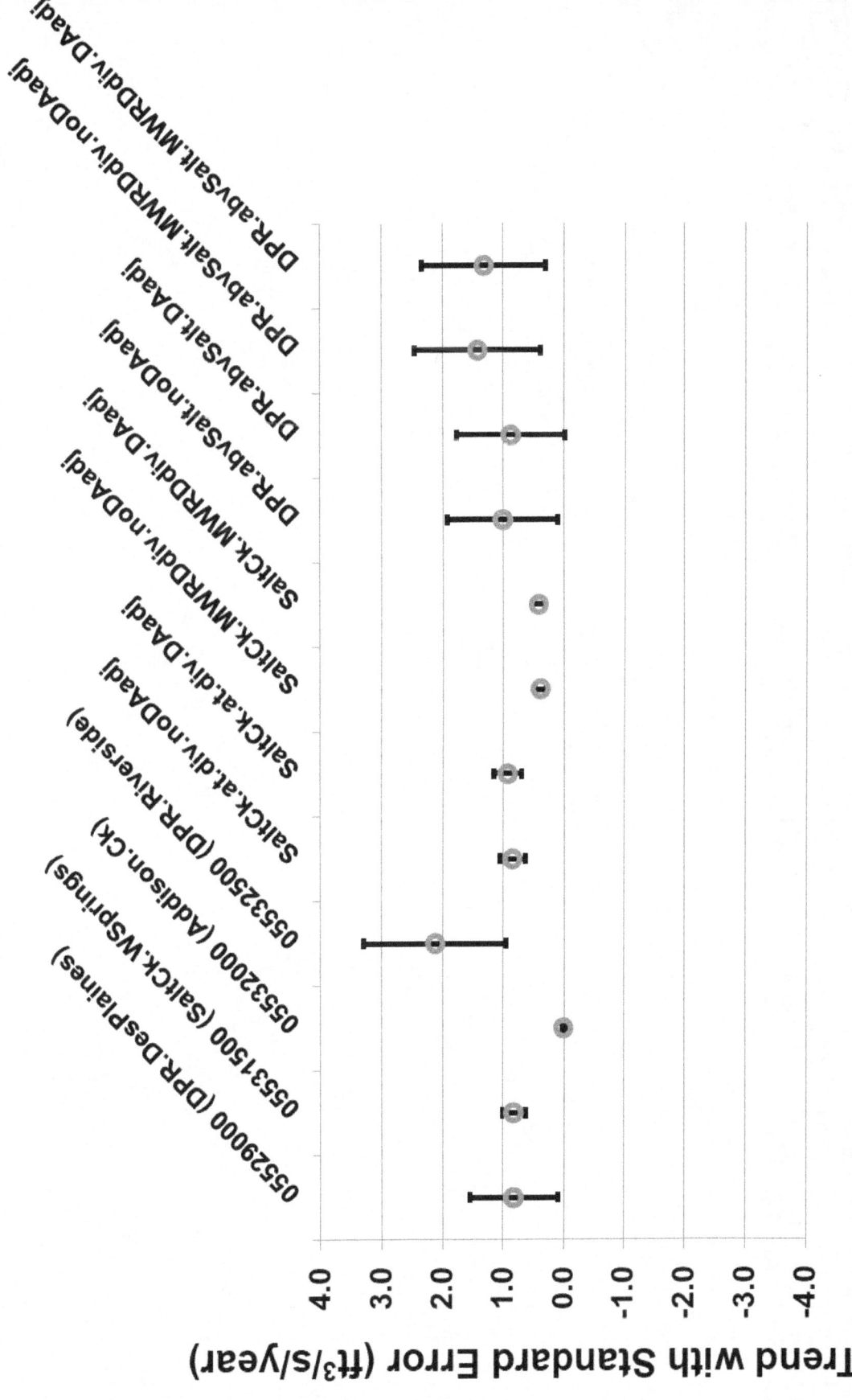

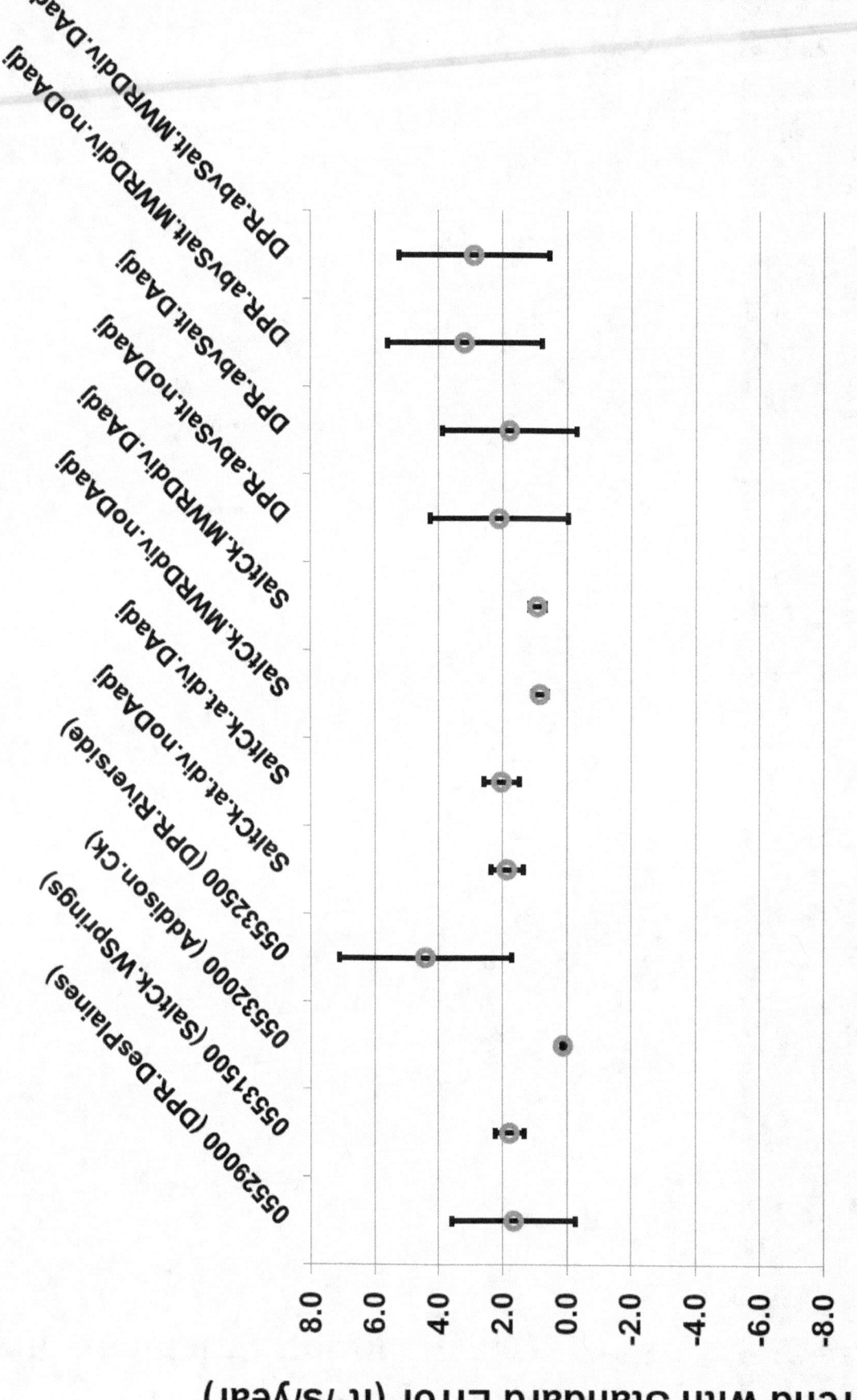

Trend Analysis: Annual Quantiles of 50%
Exceedance Daily Flow, WY 1980–2010

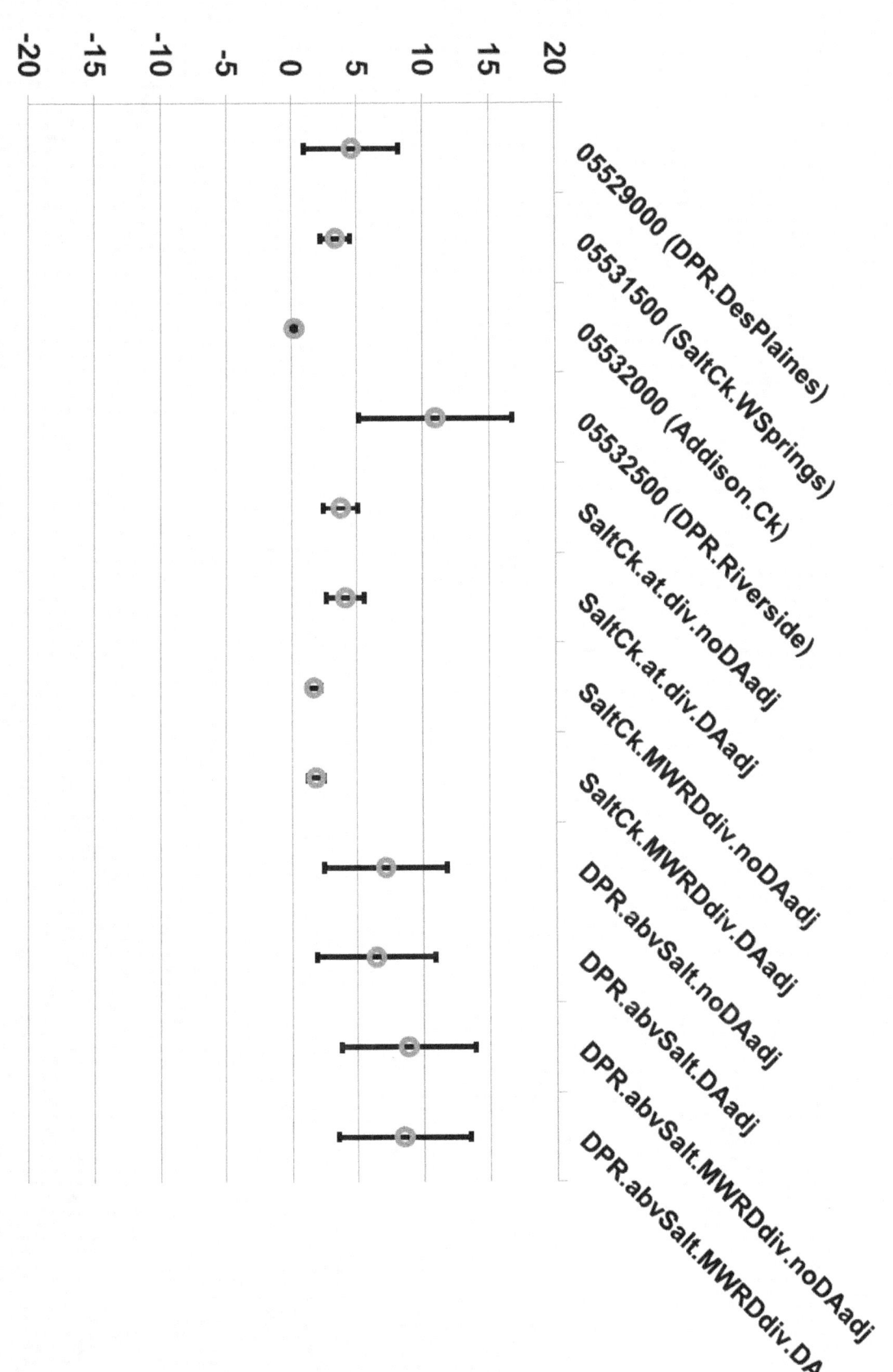

Computation of Daily Flow Quantiles: Results

Location	Applicable Des Plaines River reach	$Q_{0.80}$ (ft^3/s)	$Q_{0.50}$ (ft^3/s)	$Q_{0.20}$ (ft^3/s)
DPR.Riverside	Below Salt Ck (Reach A)	245 (246)	508 (507)	1170 (1170)
DPR.abv.SaltCk. MWRDdiv.noDAadj	Above Salt Ck, below diversion (Reach B)	199	425	1000
DPR.abv.SaltCk. MWRDdiv.DAadj	Above Salt Ck, below diversion (Reach B)	191	412	977
DPR.abv.SaltCk.no DAadj	Above Salt Ck, above diversion (Reach C) or no diversion (Reach B)	160 (161)	358 (358)	863 (863)
DPR.abv.SaltCk. DAadj		149	339	816

Note: Values in *italics* are from IDNR-OWR presentation (Sept. 2011) and were computed using data from CY2000–9. These values are included for comparison purposes only.

Hydraulic Appendix

Summary Table for 80th Percentile Flows

Location and Cross Section	Flow (ft³/s)		Top Width (ft)				Maximum Depth (ft)			
	Diversion Added	No Diversion	Diversion Added		No Diversion		Diversion Added		No Diversion	
			Existing	Project	Existing	Project	Existing	Project	Existing	Project
31st Street to 26th Street										
16197	149	149	169.60	167.53	165.48	162.06	5.33	5.18	5.07	4.88
14792	199	149	120.42	115.97	112.81	106.96	5.59	5.43	5.32	5.11
13666	199	149	90.70	86.93	87.04	82.16	3.10	2.87	2.88	2.58
12492	199	149	119.33	93.85	114.95	86.00	2.44	1.64	2.33	1.35
Average	---	---	**125.01**	**116.07**	**120.07**	**109.30**	**4.12**	**3.78**	**3.90**	**3.48**
Railroad to 31st Street										
11518	199	149	121.65	110.95	120.91	107.37	3.79	2.8	3.70	2.5
10591	199	149	95.41	78.79	94.84	70.58	3.79	2.43	3.74	2.18
9682	199	149	148.95	117.66	147.78	115.09	4.62	3.15	4.57	2.94
8907	199	149	98.48	87.51	98.17	86.26	6.24	4.73	6.21	4.53
Average	---	---	**116.12**	**98.73**	**115.43**	**94.83**	**4.61**	**3.28**	**4.56**	**3.04**
Salt Creek to Railroad										
7978	199	149	139.56	104.90	138.65	100.59	4.59	3.04	4.56	2.86
7387	199	149	115.59	80.81	114.75	79.19	4.33	2.61	4.31	2.49
6042	199	149	190.33	137.59	190.22	136.85	4.79	2.97	4.79	2.90
5688	199	149	159.61	127.52	159.59	126.43	4.12	2.24	4.11	2.20
Average	---	---	**151.27**	**112.71**	**150.80**	**110.77**	**4.46**	**2.72**	**4.44**	**2.61**
Hofmann Dam to Salt Creek										
4804	245	245	99.05	77.65	---	---	4.74	2.51	---	---
3542	245	245	94.22	57.53	---	---	6.08	3.3	---	---
2691	245	245	226.96	91.79	---	---	6.65	2.77	---	---
1682	245	245	368.43	97.33	---	---	7.86	1.42	---	---
Average	---	---	**197.17**	**81.08**	---	---	**6.33**	**2.50**	---	---

Summary Table for 50ᵗʰ Percentile Flows

Location and Cross Section	Flow (ft³/s)		Top Width (ft)				Maximum Depth (ft)			
	Diversion Added	No Diversion	Diversion Added		No Diversion		Diversion Added		No Diversion	
			Existing	Project	Existing	Project	Existing	Project	Existing	Project
31st Street to 26th Street										
16197	339	339	176.29	175.97	175.50	175.12	6.44	6.32	6.15	6.01
14792	425	339	140.29	138.57	136.32	134.25	6.64	6.50	6.33	6.16
13666	425	339	106.35	103.09	101.93	98.06	4.06	3.86	3.79	3.55
12492	425	339	135.63	125.67	132.03	119.91	3.31	2.78	3.12	2.47
Average	---	---	139.64	135.83	136.45	131.84	5.11	4.87	4.85	4.55
Railroad to 31st Street										
11518	425	339	128.41	123.39	127.04	120.97	4.61	4.00	4.44	3.7
10591	425	339	103.05	94.34	101.83	90.65	4.52	3.69	4.41	3.44
9682	425	339	160.08	143.09	158.74	137.26	5.31	4.4	5.21	4.18
8907	425	339	104.12	96.11	103.41	94.57	6.91	5.96	6.82	5.77
Average	---	---	123.92	114.23	122.76	110.86	5.34	4.51	5.22	4.27
Salt Creek to Railroad										
7978	425	339	147.86	129.23	147.27	124.11	5.22	4.24	5.16	4.06
7387	425	339	159.56	99.75	154.46	98.20	4.91	3.79	4.87	3.68
6042	425	339	199.42	155.74	199.12	152.43	5.33	4.11	5.31	4.05
5688	425	339	163.04	155.20	162.98	154.95	4.64	3.38	4.63	3.34
Average	---	---	167.47	134.98	165.96	132.42	5.03	3.88	4.99	3.78
Hofmann Dam to Salt Creek										
4804	508	508	106.22	85.36	---	---	5.19	3.63	---	---
3542	508	508	98.63	65.46	---	---	6.42	4.19	---	---
2691	508	508	239.04	108.35	---	---	6.93	3.59	---	---
1682	508	508	369.21	143.10	---	---	8.12	2.25	---	---
Average	---	---	203.28	100.57	---	---	6.67	3.42	---	---

Summary Table for 20th Percentile Flows

Location and Cross Section	Flow (ft³/s)		Top Width (ft)				Maximum Depth (ft)			
	Diversion Added	No Diversion	Diversion Added		No Diversion		Diversion Added		No Diversion	
			Existing	Project	Existing	Project	Existing	Project	Existing	Project
31st Street to 26th Street										
16197	816	816	320.33	254.84	181.93	180.06	8.3	8.19	7.92	7.79
14792	1000	816	161.14	160.37	158.56	157.64	8.45	8.32	8.03	7.88
13666	1000	816	138.03	135.98	134.81	129.50	5.78	5.60	5.41	5.20
12492	1000	816	171.67	154.94	153.20	149.31	5.05	4.76	4.73	4.39
Average	---	---	**197.79**	**176.53**	**157.13**	**154.13**	**6.90**	**6.72**	**6.52**	**6.32**
Railroad to 31st Street										
11518	1000	816	143.72	139.57	139.87	136.82	6.29	5.97	6.01	5.63
10591	1000	816	122.30	115.38	117.27	112.53	6.1	5.7	5.88	5.43
9682	1000	816	244.26	183.13	227.21	171.20	6.82	6.4	6.64	6.16
8907	1000	816	116.49	112.75	115.17	110.94	8.37	7.93	8.21	7.71
Average	---	---	**156.69**	**137.71**	**149.88**	**132.87**	**6.90**	**6.50**	**6.69**	**6.23**
Salt Creek to Railroad										
7978	1000	816	223.45	160.45	201.88	153.68	6.62	6.14	6.49	5.97
7387	1000	816	281.22	225.01	261.04	215.40	6.24	5.70	6.16	5.58
6042	1000	816	226.26	215.59	225.61	214.21	6.57	5.96	6.54	5.90
5688	1000	816	174.83	166.99	174.21	166.76	5.85	5.21	5.84	5.18
Average	---	---	**226.44**	**192.01**	**215.69**	**187.51**	**6.32**	**5.75**	**6.26**	**5.66**
Hofmann Dam to Salt Creek										
4804	1170	1170	120.58	109.93	---	---	6.24	5.42	---	---
3542	1170	1170	111.55	89.16	---	---	7.15	5.70	---	---
2691	1170	1170	249.84	141.52	---	---	7.51	4.90	---	---
1682	1170	1170	370.71	158.79	---	---	8.61	3.57	---	---
Average	---	---	**213.17**	**124.85**	---	---	**7.38**	**4.90**	---	---

Summary Table for 7Q10 Flows

Location and Cross Section	Flow (ft³/s)		Top Width (ft)				Maximum Depth (ft)			
	Diversion Added	No Diversion	Diversion Added		No Diversion		Diversion Added		No Diversion	
			Existing	Project	Existing	Project	Existing	Project	Existing	Project
31st Street to 26th Street										
16197	47.3	47.3	157.36	148.81	140.80	123.46	4.63	4.41	4.28	3.83
14792	101	47.3	102.09	96.88	92.39	85.42	4.93	4.72	4.59	4.12
13666	101	47.3	81.27	74.82	75.60	63.43	2.53	2.24	2.28	1.71
12492	101	47.3	103.56	77.36	101.90	68.16	2.05	1.03	1.98	0.71
Average	---	---	**111.07**	**99.47**	**102.67**	**85.12**	**3.54**	**3.10**	**3.28**	**2.59**
Railroad to 31st Street										
11518	101	47.3	118.73	96.78	118.24	82.43	3.43	2.07	3.37	1.56
10591	101	47.3	91.75	64.17	91.06	59.33	3.49	1.64	3.46	1.23
9682	101	47.3	141.35	108.29	140.68	103.55	4.34	2.38	4.31	2.03
8907	101	47.3	96.19	82.65	96.01	80.48	5.97	3.97	5.95	3.64
Average	---	---	**112.01**	**87.97**	**111.50**	**81.45**	**4.31**	**2.52**	**4.27**	**2.12**
Salt Creek to Railroad										
7978	101	47.3	131.85	91.15	131.34	80.92	4.33	2.31	4.31	2.00
7387	101	47.3	104.55	70.40	104.37	65.89	4.09	1.9	4.08	1.70
6042	101	47.3	187.84	129.79	187.80	128.61	4.57	2.29	4.57	2.17
5688	101	47.3	158.41	113.12	158.40	112.11	3.90	1.57	3.89	1.48
Average	---	---	**145.66**	**101.12**	**145.48**	**96.88**	**4.22**	**2.02**	**4.21**	**1.84**
Hofmann Dam to Salt Creek										
4804	131	131	95.97	72.41	---	---	4.54	1.82	---	---
3542	131	131	92.14	52.85	---	---	5.93	2.72	---	---
2691	131	131	217.97	79.90	---	---	6.51	2.25	---	---
1682	131	131	367.55	76.04	---	---	7.73	1.00	---	---
Average	---	---	**193.41**	**70.30**			**6.18**	**1.95**		

Summary of Simulated Changes in Average Top Width and Maximum Depth

Reach Location	20th Percentile Flows (project minus existing)		50th Percentile Flows (project minus existing)		80th Percentile Flows (project minus existing)		7Q10 Flows (project minus existing)	
	Average Top Width Change (ft)	Average Maximum Depth Change (ft)	Average Top Width Change (ft)	Average Maximum Depth Change (ft)	Average Top Width Change (ft)	Average Maximum Depth Change (ft)	Average Top Width Change (ft)	Average Maximum Depth Change (ft)
31st Street to 26th Street	-12.13	-0.19	-4.21	-0.27	-9.86	-0.38	-14.58	-0.56
Railroad to 31st Street	-18.00	-0.42	-10.79	-0.89	-19.00	-1.43	-27.04	-1.98
Salt Creek to Railroad	-31.30	-0.58	-33.01	-1.18	-39.30	-1.79	-46.57	-2.29
Hofmann Dam to Salt Creek	-88.32	-2.48	-102.71	-3.25	-116.09	-3.83	-123.11	-4.23

≋USGS

Selected References

- Asquith, W.H., 2012, lmomco--L-moments, trimmed L-moments, L-comoments, censored L-moments, and many distributions, in R package (version 1.6.1): Lubbock, Texas Tech University, accessed at http://www.cran.r-project.org/package=lmomco.

- Chow, V.T., 1959, Open channel hydraulics: New York, McGraw-Hill, 680 p.

- Easterling, D.R., and Peterson, T.C., 1995, A new method for detecting undocumented discontinuities in climatological time series: International Journal of Climatology, v. 15, p. 369–377.

- Illinois State Water Survey, 2003 (rev. Feb. 2003), 7-day 10-year low flows, Map 2, Northeastern Illinois Streams.

- Interagency Committee on Water Data, 1981, Guidelines for determining flood flow frequency: Bulletin 17B of the Hydrology Subcommittee, U.S. Department of the Interior, Geological Survey, Reston, Virginia [variously paged].

- Singh, K. P., and Ramamurthy, G.S., 1993, 7-day, 10-year low flows of streams in northeastern Illinois: Illinois State Water Survey Contract Report 545, 24 p.

- U.S. Army Corp of Engineers, Hydrologic Engineering Center, 2010, HEC-RAS river analysis system, hydraulic reference manual: version 4.1, various chapters plus appendixes.

- U.S. Geological Survey, Illinois StreamStats: accessed in May 2012 at http://streamstatsags.cr.usgs.gov/il_ss/default.aspx.